D1600151

CIVILITY LOST

Books by George A. Goens

Soft Leadership for Hard Times (2005)

Resilient Leadership for Turbulent Times: A Guide to Thriving in the Face of Adversity (2010)

Straitjacket: How Overregulation Stifles Creativity and Innovation in Education (2013)

The Fog of Reform: Getting Back to a Place Called School (2016)

It's Not My Fault: Victim Mentality and Becoming Response-able (2017)

Civility Lost: The Media, Politics, and Education (2019)

CIVILITY LOST

The Media, Politics, and Education

George A. Goens

ROWMAN & LITTLEFIELD
Lanham • Boulder • New York • London

Published by Rowman & Littlefield
An imprint of The Rowman & Littlefield Publishing Group, Inc.
4501 Forbes Boulevard, Suite 200, Lanham, Maryland 20706
www.rowman.com

6 Tinworth Street, London SE11 5AL, United Kingdom

British Library Cataloguing in Publication Information Available

Library of Congress Cataloging-in-Publication Data

Names: Goens, George A., author.
Title: Civility lost : the media, politics, and education / George A. Goens.
Description: Lanham, Maryland : Rowman & Littlefield, [2019] | Includes bibliographical references
    and index.
Identifiers: LCCN 2018026778 (print) | LCCN 2018043322 (ebook) | ISBN 9781475840452 (elec-
    tronic) | ISBN 9781475840438 (cloth : alk. paper)
Subjects: LCSH: Democracy and education—United States. | Civics—Study and teaching—United
    States. | Citizenship—Study and teaching—United States. | Civil society—United States.
Classification: LCC LC89 (ebook) | LCC LC89 .G62 2019 (print) | DDC 370.115—dc23
LC record available at https://lccn.loc.gov/2018026778

∞ ™ The paper used in this publication meets the minimum requirements of
American National Standard for Information Sciences Permanence of Paper for
Printed Library Materials, ANSI/NISO Z39.48-1992.

Printed in the United States of America

To grandchildren—the future is theirs if civility is
embraced and cherished:
Claire, Luke, Julia, Eddie, Jack, Callan, and Emerson

CONTENTS

PREFACE

Sometimes very minor and often humorous events highlight major and difficult issues. Going through the TSA line at the Milwaukee airport brought home, in a humorous way, what is needed in the United States.

As I waited for my briefcase and backpack to come through the TSA X-ray machine, I was watching the other travelers take their belts off, pull their laptops out of their briefcases, put their shoes on a conveyor belt along with their jackets and phones, and stand in line ready to be processed—being screened with their hands up in the air and feet planted squarely on the yellow painted footsteps of the glass-enclosed human-body-scanning machine.

I collected my briefcase, phone, keys, and fountain pens (yes, fountain pens) from the belt and started walking toward the terminal causeway. I looked up, and hanging from the ceiling was an official TSA sign: "Recombobulation Area." I actually laughed out loud and thought, *At least someone in the TSA has a sense of humor.*

But that phrase—*recombobulation*—was right on the mark. I had watched people *discombobulate*—stripping themselves of items that had to be checked. Having a designated area to recombobulate made sense.

The Milwaukee TSA recognized the discombobulation and the need to get things together again—the formal "Recombobulation Area." It struck me that the United States could use a means of recombobulation to get back together, to become whole, and to unify with our diverse colleagues, neighbors, and others.

While I found humor in that statement in Milwaukee, today's society, raucous and divisive, pits one segment of society against others. Civility is lost. The vision of America as a democratic and united nation of individuals who believe in equality, justice, and human dignity has been clouded.

Fractured and fragmented. The United States is undergoing serious splintering and separation that threatens not only relationships but also politics and society as a whole. Despite contemporary technology, communication and dialogue get lost in the fog of impulsive reactions and prejudices.

Divisions are emphasized. Disagreements turn into name-calling and castigating. Lines are drawn, and compromising or finding areas of agreement or commonality are not pursued. Issues are sharply painted in right or wrong, moral and immoral, ethical and unethical, principled and unprincipled, intelligent or unenlightened colors. Winning, not discourse or understanding, is the goal.

Individuals are fed up with politics, advertising, and deception emanating online, in newspapers and magazines, and from the mouths of elected officials, "talking heads," celebrities, and editors. Trust in major institutions has been shattered: Congress, the presidency, courts, police, schools, Hollywood, Madison Avenue, Wall Street, religion, and even the town square.

The United States has gone through similar times in the past. In the last twenty years, fragmentation has grown and is evident today in the media and politics that slice and dice citizens into demographics—gender, race, socioeconomic standing, politics, geography, generations, religion, philosophy, and a host of other categories.

Ironically, the United States' motto is *e pluribus unum*—out of many, one. While some focus on differences, the actual emphasis within society should be on unity as human beings and the common good. In real terms, while they come from different backgrounds and places, people all share the desire to fulfill their lives and those of their children and live with dignity and respect.

Philosophy, not force or fear, binds this country together. A sense of principle and wholeness connects the nation. After all, the United States was founded on specific ideas and aspirations that celebrate the sovereignty and authority of all citizens.

Education has an essential role in this unique nation built on principles, values, and dreams. The founders realized that an educated citizenry is a key requirement to address and understand issues confronting the country and to engage in a rational and civil conversation about how to address these issues.

Education must present ideas and explore civil dialogue to create understanding and bring people together around democratic principles and ethics. Governance "by the people" and "for the people" relies on citizens who have the understanding and capability to come together around democratic ideals and the common good.

This book explores the foundational principles and expectations for a democratic society, along with how differences can be clarified and discussed civilly to build respect, trust, and confidence in defining and finding solutions. Education must enable citizens of all dispositions to engage in those conversations to build greater understanding and respect, even though differences are inevitable. Finally, the major principles and values around which America is based must be examined, along with the inevitable conflict in their interpretation and application.

Citizens have responsibilities, not only to themselves and their families but also to the common good and their communities. An education must provide a comprehensive understanding of principles, values, and ethics that enable citizens to live together civilly with access to life, liberty, and the pursuit of happiness.

ACKNOWLEDGMENTS

I would like to thank Claire Bower, Julia Goens, and Eddie Goens for their contributions to this book. I also want to thank Marilyn Goens for her patience and suggestions, as well as her editing and other feedback about this book.

I

THE DISUNITING OF AMERICA

From time to time we've been tempted to believe that society has become too complex to be managed by self-rule, that government by an elite is superior to government for, by, and of the people. Well, if no one among us is capable of governing himself, then who among us has the capacity to govern someone else? All of us together, in and out of government, must bear the burden.

—President Ronald Reagan

Our Constitution is a remarkable, beautiful gift. But it's really just a piece of parchment. It has no power on its own. We, the people, give it power—with our participation, and the choices we make. Whether or not we stand up for our freedoms. Whether or not we respect and enforce the rule of law. America is no fragile thing. But the gains of our long journey to freedom are not assured.

—President Barack Obama

Democracy is not easy, and it is not simple. The battle of ideas is relentless. Special interests clash with the greater good. Politics becomes abrasive and coarse. Intolerance increases. News organizations become geared to commercial, not the public, interest. Politics becomes stymied by dogma that sacrifices compromise.

The question is: How does a society deal with change and conflict, the crush of ideas, the collision of values, and the imminent fragmenting based on politics and demographic factors? What holds a society and nation together? How can civility be maintained?

Democratic societies and cultures require actively engaged citizens at the local, state, and national levels. Citizens have serious responsibilities and commitments: an autocratic system requires only adherence and conformity with no challenges or questions. Apathy or gross cynicism weakens democracy.

Looking back in American history, many citizens believe there was unanimous agreement at the Constitutional Convention in 1787. Actually, it wasn't a social gathering of like-minded individuals with no friction or discord. Like any meeting concerned with significant choices and decisions, there was vociferous debate. Of the fifty-five delegates who attended, at the end of the session after reviewing the recommendations, 30 percent (twelve members) refused to sign it and went home.

At the conclusion of the Constitutional Convention, Benjamin Franklin, who was eighty-one years old and in poor health, had James Wilson read his speech to the delegates:

> I confess that there are several parts of this Constitution which I do not at present approve, but I am not sure I shall never approve them: For having lived long, I have experienced many instances of being obliged by better information or fuller consideration, to change opinions even on important subjects, which I once thought right, but found to be otherwise. It is therefore that the older I grow, the more apt I am to doubt my own judgment, and to pay more respect to the judgment of others.

This country's experience is filled with creative tension as differences and antagonism arise. Major issues do not have a single perspective or simplistic answers. Conflicting facts, contrary interpretations, and distinct philosophical positions raise questions and complexity.

Any discussion about improving society arouses opposition and differences. Debate is essential, but vitriol toward individuals with different points of view has no place. Fellow citizens are not enemies simply because they have diverse ideas, philosophies, or interpretations. Debate and deliberation are not contrary to a good social order; they are actually prerequisites for democracy and the possibility of a better future.

THWARTING DEMOCRACY

Democracy works best with the open expression of ideas. The issues are complicated, and simple answers are not always evident. In some cases, they are nonexistent. Values and ethics are involved, and sometimes even a clash of positive ideals and rights occur (for example, the clash of privacy and national security). While Americans value their privacy, they also value their security and that of their families.

Discussion and debate over racism, free speech, abortion, affirmative action, healthcare, and many other issues arouse public confrontations in the national and social media. Issues are problematic, and difficult questions are posed and debate ensues from a variety of perspectives.

The question is how these interactions are conducted. In some cases, differences are highlighted and citizens disassociate from those with divergent opinions or philosophies. Breaches and detachment eliminate any possibility to comprehend and understand the position of others.

People retreat and create an "us versus them" mentality, withdrawing into silos with people of like views, away from "elites," "deplorables," or other negative classification of those with different perspectives. They, of course, believe their view is the "true" interpretation—the others are false.

Individuals or groups begin to perceive those who disagree with them as enemies. "I would never work with any of those people" or "I don't ever want anything to do with you." "You're a bigot, racist, wingnut, radical, ideologue." Epithets like these push the plausibility of a dialogue beyond reason and reality.

When this happens, polarization occurs and mistrust grows, and a vacuum results. Individuals stop talking and discussing issues and lose opportunities to consider other concepts and reasoning. Even public opinion polls have not accurately depicted citizens' attitudes because of the wariness of individuals to publicly and explicitly detail their personal perspectives and opinions.

Confronting issues and facing conflict, particularly if principles and values are involved, is stressful. Emotions soar, and logic and reason become victim to anger and malice. In some cases, individuals take things personally, as though a disagreement about ideas is an assault on their intelligence or character.

In his book *Flow*, Csikszentmihalyi[1] indicated that there are two ways people respond to personal or societal stress. The positive response is "transformational coping"; the negative reaction is "neurotic defense."

A neurotic defense is to withdraw, stop being involved, and deny any involvement or responsibility for what has occurred or is unfolding. Turning against and blaming others is a part of this position.

A more mature approach is to suppress anger, name-calling, and aggression and reassess circumstances by analyzing situations logically and analytically. This position can create a transformation of responses and circumstances and build greater insight and connection.

Unfortunately, often individuals, groups, and media personalities take the "neurotic" approach, dividing and polarizing individuals into good or bad groups. People who feel castigated or insecure withdraw, eliminating the possibility of mutual insight or comprehension. Barriers are formed.

Democracy weakens when individuals talk only to those with whom they agree: the center of society splinters and civic responsibility deteriorates. Networks of community organizations with diverse interests break apart, and people stop working to find common ground.

When this happens, solutions are not discovered and differences are reinforced negatively, and a dangerous cycle of indifference can begin. In many cases, people disengage and look to others to take control and determine what to do. Frustration, isolation, and contempt are contrary to democratic values and meeting the civic duties of citizenship.

FRACTURES AND FISSURES

George Washington in 1796 foresaw the impact of polarization on democracy. Specifically, he was wary of political parties and the "baneful effects of the spirit of party." He warned of

> the alternate domination of one faction over another, sharpened by the spirit of revenge natural to party dissention, which in different ages & countries has perpetrated the most horrid enormities, is itself a frightful despotism. But this leads at length to a more formal and permanent despotism. The disorders & miseries, which result, gradually incline the minds of men to seek security & repose in the absolute power of an Individual: and or later the chief of some prevailing faction more able

or more fortunate than his competitors, turns this disposition to the purposes of his own elevation, on the ruins of Public Liberty.[2]

Other presidents emphasized that democracy requires basic solidarity. Periods of national crisis brought people together in common purpose. *E pluribus unum* is an ideal most politicians support. In crisis situations, citizens unite under one banner and forget their political, economic, and social differences. The call to unite and face the state of affairs bonds individuals in a sense of community.

Historically, Americans have been optimists. The American Dream lives in the hearts of most citizens. They work individually and hope their children's lives are better than theirs and that their future is filled with success and meaning. While we celebrate individualism, a sense of community and national spirit brings people together. Collectively, Americans are a "can do" people, up to challenges: being united in overcoming challenges is part of the nation's story.

Westward expansion, the fight for liberty and justice, facing worldwide challenge of economic depression and foreign wars, and expecting and producing economic and social growth are all symbolic, unifying struggles. However, everything was not achieved with storybook ease. Conflict was apparent, but out of the challenges creative solutions and endeavors emerged.

A sense of purpose is the glue that unites people in community. Americans believe that as a nation they are committed to something exceptional—freedom, equality, democracy, individualism, and rule of law. They trust that progress and success are achievable: the American flag planted on the moon has been symbolic of the country's commitment to defining and achieving difficult goals.

The nation's stories are a unique combination of individualism and a sense of community and unity. Betty Sue Flowers wrote, "We need a new myth that takes into account our diversity but makes it coherent—one that allows us to stick together in the name of a higher ideal and to work for a common good but at the same time to celebrate our individuality. We need a higher organization of our complexity. We need a new myth of who we are—and who we might be."[3]

SLICING AND DICING

Working for a common ideal is a powerful unifier. The application of individual abilities in common cause coalesces commitment. American ideals of democracy, liberty, and equality bring people together, unifying their spirit and effort. The country's identity is based around the dedication to those core values, which is, in reality, the foundation of a civil society.

But there are issues. The generic term *American* has been demographically sliced and hyphenated into geographic, economic, racial, gender, educational, religious, and political descriptors. Certainly, to improve overall conditions, examining the impact on individual groups and segments of society make some sense.

The rise of identity politics, however, has created division; sometimes pitting the perceived good for one group against the needs of others. In some cases, politicians try to stitch together enough votes for victory by dividing, not unifying, society around an ideal or ethic.

Today, the dicing of people into demographic and special interest groups plays into the self-interest mode. Differences, not connections, are highlighted, and, at times, some segments critique and condemn other competing groups or interests. Perceiving individuals through a demographic lens artificially separates people into singular categories as if they were not simply people—Americans with common interests, dreams, and principles.

In politics, pundits analyze candidates and issues based on their impact groups or identities and other data-collection silos. The media and politicians then categorize issues into women's issues, minority issues, LGBTQ issues, white-collar or blue-collar issues, urban issues, rural issues—ad nauseam. Fragmenting people is a serious problem.

Instead of citizens seeing issues in terms of principle—justice or equality—they are labeled by gender or race or another demographic. Some may feel that because they are not part of the identified group that the issue does not concern them. If they are simply stated as issues of justice, equality, goodness, freedom, truth, and liberty, all citizens should be aware and concerned. These are universal ideals and values in America. Principles and values are universal, and if one person is denied them, it is everyone's concern.

The United States is a diverse nation united by noble values and principles expressed in and protected by the Bill of Rights and the Constitution, which are not frozen in time. Change in the United States has come through a commitment to pursue the ideals in these documents and make them a reality for all.

Arthur Schlesinger Jr., a historian and an advisor to President John F. Kennedy, worked with politicians and the Democratic Party throughout his career and became a noted public intellectual. Schlesinger expressed concern in his book, *The Disuniting of America*, about the divisions that were occurring in the country.

> Instead of a nation composed of individuals making their own unhampered choices, America increasingly sees itself as composed of groups more or less ineradicable in their ethnic character. The multi ethnic dogma abandons historic purpose, replacing assimilation by fragmentation, integration by separation. It belittles unum and glorifies pluribus.[4]

He asserted that this view considers America not as a nation of individuals, but a nation of groups classified by "ethnic and racial criteria." As a result, "the historic theory of America as one people" that kept American "society whole" is being reversed.

While the United States is diverse, it has a unique "national character"[5] developed through common ideals. Polarization into demographic or other categories comes with the cost of less cohesion and unity, and ultimately less stability. Diversity does not have to come at the price of unity.

INDIVIDUALISM

Alexis de Tocqueville indicated that Americans have the habit of "individualism," which he described as "a calm and considered feeling which disposes each citizen to isolate himself from the mass of his fellows and withdraw into the circle of family and friends; with their little society formed to his face, he gladly leaves the greater society to look after itself."[6]

Individualism is a positive trait, but if it weakens our "communal fabric," it can slip into self-centeredness and selfishness.[7] Communalism and individualism are both evident in a democracy and can be balanced so individual expression and the common good can be nurtured.

Politics requires the creativity of a diverse society and an ability to interact with each other and find shared interests, needs, and outcomes. Getting individuals and local communities to focus on common goals has always been a powerful force for change, although not an easy achievement. Centralized, top-down dictums generally fail and create greater conflict.

Extreme polarization and withdrawal of individuals lead to centralization of power with the danger of despotism. Centralized power, in fact, leaves people more isolated. According to Levin, "The distinctive political failures of our era are functions of increasing centralized administration in an increasingly decentralized society."[8]

Greater centralization is the father of conformity, with individuals facing retribution and castigation if they do not comply. Conformity pulls people to following group norms because of the desire for acceptance and security within the larger group. Attraction for acceptance leads to disastrous results.

WHAT CITIZENS MUST KNOW

- Conflict and disagreement are prevalent in a democracy and require citizens to be engaged actively at the national, state, and local levels.
- Free speech and expression are rights. Issues are complex and sometimes divisive, which can cause fragmentation and discord.
- All citizens must comprehend American history and its democratic foundations, principles, and values.
- As polarization deepens, people often resort to labeling, and they cease to engage in discussion and deliberation with others.
- A sense of purpose and commitment to ideas is a powerful force that can unite people and communities.
- Polarization comes at a cost of lost cohesion, unity, and purpose.
- Principles and values unite all citizens: finding common ground is essential to make progress.

NOTES

1. Mihaly Csikszentmihalyi, *Flow* (New York: HarperCollins, 2008), 199.

2. George Washington Farewell Address, 1796, http://gwpapers.virginia.edu/documents_gw/farewell/transcript.html.

3. Betty Sue Flowers, "American Dream and the Economic Myth," *Essays on Deepening the American Dream*, Fetzer Institute (Spring 2007), Essay no. 12, 31.

4. Arthur M. Schlesinger, *The Disuniting of America: Reflections on a Multicultural Society*, revised and enlarged edition (New York: W. W. Norton, 2007), 21.

5. Schlesinger, *The Disuniting of America*, 20.

6. Parker J. Palmer, *Healing the Heart of Democracy: The Courage to Create a Politics Worthy of the Human Spirit* (Hoboken, NJ: Wiley, 2014), 41.

7. Palmer, *Healing the Heart of Democracy*, 43.

8. Yuval Levin, *The Fractured Republic* (New York: Basic Books).

2

MEDIA AND POLITICAL PARTIES

Those who expect to reap the blessings of freedom must undergo the fatigue of supporting it.

—Thomas Paine, 1777

Over the years the media—broadcasting, publishing, and the internet—brought about significant changes in accessing information. In the past, newspapers, radio, and the thirty-minute evening telecasts were the mainstays of news and updates.

Today communication has expanded as the internet allows for constant and almost instant interaction through email, text, and social sites. As a seventy-year-old gentleman said, "Kids are texting constantly. I tell them that texts are nothing more that electronic telegrams except they come instantaneously, and you do not have to say 'stop' at the end each sentence. Some wonder what a telegram is."

Technology has altered access to news. Newspapers, prevalent in the 1950s and 1960s, had to face and compete with twenty-four-hour news on television and radio. They reduced staff as circulation became a struggle, and many local newspapers shut down. Today major papers are online and compete with "publications" geared to specific political or philosophical perspectives, slants, and audiences. The web has round-the-clock programming, and the once major news stations like ABC, CBS, and NBC face a wide variety of competitive sources outside the traditional mainstream.

What has happened is "narrowcasting," not broadcasting. Now Americans talk past each other and retire into their media "echo chambers," reading only articles or pieces that agree with their politics and philosophy. Besides the "echo chamber" sources, citizens confront other challenges.

What is presented sometimes succumbs to a "if it bleeds, it leads" approach in determining what gets reported. Substantive issues fall victim to sensational stories, scandal, and "infotainment." Selective images are used in quick sound bites to highlight stories. Ratings and sales are important, directing what and how things are covered. Longer in-depth pieces do not get aired. Complicated issues cannot get adequate and appropriate coverage in three-minute segments or short interview clips.

The *Columbia Journalism Review* examined the nature of press coverage of the candidates in the 2016 presidential election. The study found that stories in the last three months of the campaign concerned candidates' personal issues and scandals, which far exceeded any coverage of policy or other issues.

While policy is a critical factor to voters in supporting candidates, the study found, "In light of the stark policy choices facing voters in the 2016 election, it seems incredible that only 5 out of 150 front-page articles that *The New York Times* ran over the last, most critical months of the election, attempted to compare the candidate's policies, while only 10 described the policies of either candidate in any detail."[1]

Another study by the Shorenstein Center on Media, Politics and Public Policy basically agreed with the *Columbia* study. Both candidates "received coverage that was overwhelmingly negative in tone and extremely light on policy."[2] This is a trend since the 1980s. Incessant criticism has a "corrosive effect" and erodes trust in political leaders and institutions. Negativity in coverage is necessary at times, unless it overwhelms reporting on policy analysis and other essential areas.

Citizens rely on the press and journalism for their information on elections and other important issues. Lack of policy coverage and overwhelming emphasis on scandal and the election "horse race" aspect deprives the citizenry of important information necessary to become well educated about the issues.

The availability and avalanche of media sites and reports cause some people to simply justify their views or to withdraw entirely from media and discussions. The so-called information overload can provoke a retreat and separation from civic and political affairs. A cadre of political or philosophical shows, complete with a stable of "talking heads," presents a one-viewpoint perspective shouting down contrary views. Mass media are products of corporate profits and agendas that may not be congruent with meeting the needs of the public interest.

Good journalism is important in a democracy, but, at times, it may be the victim of partisan or political self-interest. As a result, citizens mistrust the media.

> The media has not been able to maintain its reputation for fairness in the wake of its own problem with journalists who plagiarize and television stations that become cheerleaders for political causes. No wonder that when it comes to the most important institution of all, at least for the purposes of realizing what holds us together and defines us as a collective identity, Americans express such distrust in government.[3]

Highly respected journalists have raised issues about television and its impact on society. In a speech at Duke University in 1987, Ted Koppel stated, "You won't be surprised to learn that there is not a great deal of room on television for complexity. We are nothing, as an industry, if not attuned to the appetites and limitations of our audience. We have learned, for example, that your attention span is brief. We should know; we helped make it that way."[4]

Koppel declared that television and complexity seldom mix. He went on to say, "We require nothing of you; only to watch or say that you are watching if Mr. Nielsen's representatives should happen to call." Truth, he added, is not a polite tap on the shoulder but strong medicine that many do not want to hear.

News and reporting have been "dumbed down" with an emphasis on human interest, sensationalism, and shallowness. The result is a blitz of "disinformation, infotainment, and opinion that presents itself as information."[5] Distinguishing fact from fiction and truth from opinion are critical and very necessary skills in today's world. The present challenge, as in the past, is having the intellectual skills to do so.

Tom Fenton, former senior foreign correspondent for CBS, remarked that the networks failed to warn the citizenry about the "storm clouds" in the Middle East approaching the American shores. "In failing to do so, we betrayed the trust of the public."[6] In the three months leading up to the 9/11 attack, al-Qaeda was not mentioned once in the three major evening news broadcasts.

He attributes this phenomenon to corporations taking over major news companies; as a result, costs squeezed the life out of foreign news reporting. Corporate greed and profit reduced foreign news coverage because of its price tag. As a result, the public was not fully informed of the foreign affairs that eventually led to war.

Executives, editors, and producers believe the public cannot digest much hard news, particularly concerning foreign affairs. Instead, they prefer providing simplified information because they feel intelligent news will mean lower ratings and financial loss.

Fenton goes on to say, "Politicians and the media have conspired to infantilize, to dumb down, the American public. At heart, politicians don't believe that Americans can handle complex truth, and the news media, especially television, basically agrees."[7]

Fenton cited the reasons for television's approach to the news. Obviously, news as a profit center is a major factor, along with the expense of foreign bureaus and an obsession with ratings. In addition, the deregulation of broadcasting and the decline of the code of standards is the result, in part, of the competition for ratings that is the consequence of "soft" and fear-based news attitudes about telecasts.

The Pew Research Center[8] conducted research on the attitudes of Americans concerning the media. Newspaper readership is down 8 percent, while cable and morning network television is up 10 percent and 14 percent, respectively. With Democrats and those who lean Democratic, 46 percent indicate the media has a negative effect on the country, while 85 percent of the Republicans and those who lean Republican hold this negative perspective.

POLITICAL PARTIES

Differences between the two parties exist, as always, but now they are very pronounced. Opinions of other national institutions illustrate significantly different views by Democrats and Republicans. The percentage of Democrats and Republicans who hold a favorable perception regarding church/religious organizations, banks/financial institutions, labor unions, and colleges and universities are listed on the next page.

Republicans and Democrats differ significantly on attitudes toward religion, unions, national media, and colleges and universities. In some

Percent Positive Perception

	Republicans	Democrats
Churches/religious organizations	73%	50%
Banks/financial	46%	33%
Labor unions	33%	59%
National media	10%	44%
Colleges/universities	36%	72%

cases, both parties are on the negative side of the ledger (for example, banks/financial institutions and national media).

The perspectives of the political parties clash, creating conflict in policy, philosophy, and social priorities as well as governing strategies. However, in the past even in difficult times the ability to find compromise was possible. Today a change in how members of each major party portrays the other exemplifies the growing negative approach that leads to deep divisions and affects the ability to find solutions.

The Pew Research Center[9] found that both Democrats and Republicans perceive each other's policies beyond simply "dislike," to the point of labeling them a threat to "the nation's well-being." Among Republicans, 68 percent say that the Democratic policies are "harmful to the country," and 62 percent of Democrats believe Republican policies "harm the country." Partisan polarization has grown and expanded to mutual contempt for the opposing party.

When a majority of Democrats and Republicans perceive members of the other party as close-minded threats and when more than 40 percent perceive members of the other party as dishonest, compromise is difficult, if not impossible. Some 62 percent of Republicans and 58 percent of Democrats believe that compromise should come on their own party's terms and that their party should get more of what it wants. With this attitude, compromise is not striking a balance but simply focuses on defeating the other side and winning.

The result of these party perspectives is ideological "silos" in which both liberals and conservatives, Republicans and Democrats, live. This indicates that they would rather associate with people with similar perspectives and philosophies than engage with those with other viewpoints.

Perceiving people in the other party as immoral creates breaches that are difficult to overcome. Some 47 percent of Republicans see Democrats as immoral, and 35 percent of Democrats perceive Republicans as immoral. These attitudes certainly do not make for bipartisanship or cooperation when the trust level is so low. It is ironic that people elected to public office to solve problems and work across the aisle retreat into party cocoons and perceive a significant percentage of members of the other party as being morally questionable.

Americans overall describe themselves collectively very positively: 79 percent reported that Americans are patriotic, 69 percent perceive them to be honest, and 67 percent describe them as intelligent. On the other side of the ledger, concerning Americans' negative traits: 68 percent say selfish and 50 percent indicate lazy. In addition to how Americans perceive fellow citizens, individuals generally have less confidence in elected officials: 55 percent believe that "ordinary Americans" would do a better job than their elected officials. [10]

In the mid-1990s, *Washington Post* columnist David Broder stated, "Cynicism is epidemic right now. It saps people's confidence in politics and public officials, and it erodes both the standing and standards of journalism. If the assumption is that nothing is on the level, nothing is what it seems, then citizenship becomes a game for fools, and there is no point in trying to stay informed." [11]

The polarization of politicians and the purification of parties ideologically is messy and creates disconnection. Socially, we have been divided by a variety of demographic labels. What is lost in this slicing and dicing of Americans is a commitment to the country's stated values under which democracy must operate. Labels separate. Values and principles bring people together. Ideas have the power to unify because they promote discussion and thought, assuming that the environment and culture allows such interaction and relationships.

In 1979, President Jimmy Carter gave an address that was criticized as the "malaise" speech, even though he never used the word. Times were tough: inflation, energy problems, Watergate, and the end of Richard Nixon's failed presidency. The attitude of citizens was negative, morale suffered, and confidence was waning.

President Carter warned that the United States was at a turning point and that overworked Americans had a choice. "One is a path I've warned about tonight, the path that leads to fragmentation and self-interest. Down that road lies a mistaken idea of freedom, the right to grasp for ourselves some advantage over others. That path would be one of constant conflict between narrow interests ending in chaos and immobility. It is a certain route to failure."[12] He indicated that the second path is "of common purpose and restoration of American values": commitment to work collectively as a nation to address issues. Carter's insight would be appropriate today.

Fragmentation and fractures do not happen overnight: as in the past, they grow from broken dreams and promises, lost respect when deeds do not match words, and when government and institutions do not act with integrity and address the needs of people and the challenges facing them. Integrity to values and trust are powerful forces in bringing people together. Without integrity, the ability to listen to each other and unite in the common good is lost.

WHAT CITIZENS MUST KNOW

- The media has had a major impact on access to information, the nature of information provided, and the complexity of information—all driven by ratings and profitability.
- Individual ideological "silos" reinforce division and do not provide for the presentation of alternative viewpoints and the ability to come together and address issues.
- The polarization of politicians and the purification of political parties ideologically create dissension, stalemate, and lack of compromise.
- Loss of integrity in the media and politicians results in a loss of optimism and civility.

NOTES

1. Duncan J. Watts and David M. Rothschild, "Don't Blame the Election on Fake News. Blame It on the Media," *Columbia Journalism Review*, December 5, 2017, https://www.cjr.org/analysis/fake-news-media-election-trump.php.

2. Thomas E. Patterson, "News Coverage of the 2016 General Election: How the Press Failed the Voters," Shorenstein Center on Media, Politics and Public Policy, December 7, 2016, 9, https://shorensteincenter.org/news-coverage-2016-general-election/.

3. Alan Wolfe, *Return to Greatness* (Princeton, NJ: Princeton University Press, 2005), 194.

4. Ted Koppell, Commencement Address, Duke University, Durham, North Carolina, May 10, 1987, https://duke.edu/ark:/87924/r4d21rz7w.

5. Parker J. Palmer, *Healing the Heart of Democracy: The Courage to Create a Politics Worthy of the Human Spirit* (Hoboken, NJ: Wiley, 2014), 152.

6. Tom Fenton, *Bad News: The Decline of Reporting, the Business of News, and the Danger to Us All* (New York: HarperCollins, 2005), 3.

7. Fenton, *Bad News*, 85.

8. Pew Research Center, "Sharp Partisan Divisions in Views of National Institutions," October 7, 2017, http://www.people-press.org/2017/07/10/sharp-partisan-divisions-in-views-of-national-institutions/.

9. Pew Research Center, "Partisanship and Political Animosity in 2016," http://www.people-press.org/2016/06/22/partisanship-and-political-animosity-in-2016/.

10. Pew Research Center, "Patriotic, Honest, and Selfish: How Americans Describe . . . Americans," November 2015, http://www.pewresearch.org/fact-tank/2015/12/11/patriotic-honest-and-selfish-how-americans-describe-americans/.

11. Patterson, "News Coverage of the 2016 General Election," 18.

12. Jimmy Carter, "The Public Papers of the Presidents, 1977" (Washington, DC: Government Publishing Office, 1978, 1980).

3

THE COMMON GOOD

What are the American ideals? They are the development of the individual for his own and the common good; the development of the individual through liberty; and the attainment of the common good through democracy and social justice.

—Justice Louis Brandeis

Societal change is inevitable. Some calm the waters, and others create waves of discord and confusion. Transitions can be unsettling as the unknown creates uncertainty and anxiety. Change plays out slowly, raising doubts and questions, even with its advocates.

Coming to terms with what is emerging is not always straightforward because of the fears people have personally and socially. Losses and gains and opportunities and restrictions slowly unfold. Change can produce solutions to issues and problems and reshape circumstances, easing the landscape for compromise and new beginnings. At times, however, things are thrown askew, raising pressures and escalating divisions because of real or perceived outcomes.

Individuals who sense change as jeopardizing their goals and ambitions resort to "conflict behavior in order to achieve their goals."[1] As a consequence, this behavior can bring about intense disagreements and animosity. People feel they must protect and defend themselves because they perceive a threat to their family, employment, community, or future.

Social and political change frequently follows this pattern: an alteration in structure or situation leads to a change in behavior and a corresponding modification in attitude, which results in friction and opposition. Trust lessens, and the possibility of respectful discussion diminishes. Polarization along with mobilization occurs, which takes the conflict to a higher level.

Not all change has similar characteristics. Some produce new conflicts, and others intensify existing conflicts. On the other side of the coin, others can reduce conflict, make it less severe, or actually help settle it. Some change brings about unforeseen evolution: unanticipated results and obstacles come to the fore that were not perceived previously.

All change, however, is not of the same magnitude. Mitchell[2] identifies several types of change some will experience at some point in their life. Changes can be major in scope and intensity, and others may occur abruptly and totally unexpectedly with no prior indication of its possibility. Some occur gradually, while others accelerate in a short time span.

Changes and cycles create apprehension and anxiety for some to the extent that they cut themselves off from events physically and emotionally. They separate and withdraw. Others act out more aggressively and enter the fray as assertively as they can. Loss and gain can both be stressful. Events have personal as well as community repercussions, sometimes simultaneously.

People act and ask, "What's in it for me?" or "How does this affect my family?" Self-interest can spawn narrow vision, short-term efforts, and aggression regardless of the implications for others.

Society is filled with a bit of self-centeredness. Technology promotes an egocentric culture of likes and the constant barking of exploits and achievements. Narcissism is a result of a celebrity culture and the helicopter parenting style that deflects responsibility and obligation and celebrates ego. In addition, victim mentality stymies being response-able and can result in learned helplessness and passive aggressive behavior.[3]

How can society confront the changes technologically, politically, and socially in a way that is good for the whole—the common good? Coming together, not separating, is an underwritten value of the United States. The common good is a principle that promotes individual self-realization but also the formulation of a society and culture that serves the greater public interest.

CENTRIPETAL AND CENTRIFUGAL FORCES

In society, as in physics, there are forces that hold things together and forces that pull things apart. Sir Isaac Newton describes centripetal force as one by which bodies are drawn or impelled to a center point, whereas a centrifugal force draws a body away from the center point.

In contemporary times, centrifugal forces work to destabilize society and government by creating sects or special interest groups, cutting individuals into negative factions. These forces can destroy civil conversation and dialogue.

With centrifugal forces, individuals retreat and engage in groupthink around binary assumptions that split people into positive and negative categories. The core forces that unite people become weakened as people are pulled away.

By contrast, centripetal forces bind people together and provide the strength and resilience necessary to respond to difficult times. A major centripetal unifying force in the United States is the country's basic principles and core values—life, liberty, justice, and equality. They create a compelling collective motivational force for positive change and the improvement of lives. They are forces that address people's lives individually and collectively.

The compulsion of society and systems of justice united around the concepts of freedom and equality coalesce citizens around constructive change. Forces for good connect people. External threats to national values have been uniting forces pulling the nation together as it came to grips with the larger world and its threatening impact on American life and governance.

The divisions today are not unique. Factions existed from the country's inception. John Haidt,[4] professor of ethical leadership at New York University, stated that polarization ebbs and flows. Developing simplistic binary thought—good versus bad, enemies versus friends, enlightened versus deplorables—has a dogmatic and anti-intellectual appeal.

This is contrary to Martin Luther King's call to end segregation and racism by bonding together as a nation through the values under which the country was formed. In this case, King used values, not strict power and force, as the centripetal force to bring about transformation.

Education must open the eyes of students to something greater than a simplistic binary thought process of good or bad. Reason and reflection are necessary to understand the complexities and undercurrents that affect and create questions and issues. As Thomas Jefferson stated, "For here we are not afraid to follow the truth wherever it may lead, nor tolerate any errors as long as reason is left free to combat it." Values and reason are essential for people to find pathways to progress.

THE COMMONS

The concept of the common good emanates from Western political philosophy. Aristotle expressed issues of the common good as opposed to matters of the "rulers good." Rousseau asserted that the "general will" is separate from the will of individuals or groups. The general will requires reflecting on the sense of justice for individuals and society as a whole. In a democratic society, government must follow the will of the people.

The United States does not have divine rights of royalty, theocracy, or totalitarianism. It is founded on Western political thought as evident in the Constitution and its organization, system, and controls. The common good concerns ensuring that the "social policies, social institutions, and environments on which we depend are beneficial to all."[5]

The common good, nationally or locally, involves extensive commitments and responsibilities of both government and citizens. As a matter of principle, Americans are not isolated but engaged civilly and personally in community. As an ideal, the commons conveys "a sense of an irreducibly shared life within a manageable frame."[6]

Historically, the commons were a meeting place. Citizens came to the village green to bank, shop, worship, and conduct public business, as well as obtain services from doctors, lawyers, and others. The commons were a place for education at the local schoolhouse, checking books out at the library, enjoying celebrations and memorials, and, of course, engaging in politics. People came together at the green in a sense of shared purpose and life.

Community is where individuals and families spend most of their time. Everyone remembers the neighborhood in which they were raised: bound together, sharing space, responsibilities, and resources as part of community living and citizenship. People belong to communities because cooperation and generosity are important to them.

The commons symbolically emphasized a shared life connected by a common culture, language, and history. The commons are derived from the legal term for common land, belonging equally and shared by the entire community. It is representative of a local unified system and society.

The concern for the welfare of the community is called the commonweal. The commonweal pertains to the general welfare of the public: the happiness, safety, and security of the people in the community or the greater nation. The commonweal is considered the "public good" because people work for shared ideals and principles in common cause. This can be done while still valuing and celebrating individualism: they are not mutually exclusive. In society people can be both independent and interdependent under these values and address individual as well as collective needs.

A shared sense of belonging and connection comes from a commitment to the principles of a democratic and civil society. Communities care for the well-being of citizens. The common good concerns the benefit and interests of the people—society as a whole—and is different and sometimes opposed to self-interest, special interests, or the private good of individuals or corporations. The common good coalesces individuals to participate and use their individual talents and freedom on behalf of all.

Without the idea of the common good, society can become atomized with individuals detached from each other, which can deteriorate the footings of a civil society. The common good aims for government and citizens to take collective action in the care of the overall community and general public.

People cherish their individual freedom, and they do not want anything restricting the pursuit of their purpose and passions. "Don't tread on me" does not ring hollow when individuals are involved with their personal interests and security. Working for self or selfish interests alone, however, does not fulfill the role of citizen. The liberties of the greater society enable individuals to pursue their interests. In return, citizens must meet their civic duties to ensure those liberties.

Getting people to abandon their exclusive goals for an abstract common good is not easy. In many cases, individuals will not achieve any personal benefit from those proposals. For example, public service and the military are focused beyond self-interest to the collective welfare of the nation. Security and justice are not products of self-interest. They can be achieved only through collective commitment and action, requiring the participation of the common citizen. Public education is a public good all citizens must support to ensure a viable democracy.

The concepts of self-government, shared meaning and purpose, and commitment and service are focused on cohesion for collective action for "good." Cohesion is nurtured through quality relationships and fostered through awareness and obligation.

Communication and ongoing dialogue are essential to develop leadership and active citizenship that enhances the common good. Barbara Crosby and John Bryson specify that "the common good entails widely beneficial outcomes that are never preordained but instead arrived at through mindful leadership and followership. We describe the desired outcomes of leadership for the common good as a regime of mutual gain, a system of policies, programs, laws, rules and norms that yield widespread benefits at reasonable cost and taps people's deepest interests in their own well-being and that of others."[7]

All of this requires active citizens. Acting for the common good requires resolve and patience. Common threads, relationships, and themes must be found around which people can unify and act. Clarifying the importance of the common good between groups and stakeholders leads to determining the action to accomplish it.

Interpretations of concepts may and will differ, raising conjecture and debate. Even concepts like the common good, the commons, and the commonweal may have different interpretations. Concepts such as public interest, public good, or a just society can be defined differently and viewed cynically or positively.

Potential solutions require discussion and clarifying perspectives on what is unimportant and what is imperative. The time frame for showing results, tangible or otherwise, is longer than people desire or expect. Uncertainty and conflict and gains and losses are a part of civic and community actions and life.

Leadership necessary to make progress on the common good requires a sense of political efficacy. Simply stated, it is an individual's confidence that they are capable to take part in politics and circumstances— confidence that they can have a voice and that officials and others will listen and respond.[8]

The leadership may be formal, with individuals assuming stipulated or governmental roles, or it can be informal, arising from the citizenry or groups seeing the need. Informal power can be as strong and effective as formal power.

Political efficacy must be coupled with a sense of purpose. Anyone assuming leadership must understand introspectively why they want to act and/or lead. If it is simply self-serving and manipulative, then it is hollow and unable to capture other people's imaginations or commitment.

Basically, Burns states, "Authentic leadership is a collective process . . . and it emerges from the clash and congruence of motives and goals of leaders and followers. It requires neither that leaders slavishly adapt their own motives and goals to those of followers nor vice versa. It means that, in the reaching out by leaders to potential followers, broader and higher ranges of motivation come into play and that both goals and means of achieving them are informed by the force of higher end-values and modal values."[9]

A community's demeanor is emblematic of its character and commitment to values. As with individuals, character defines the nature of relationships, goals and interactions, and the operational culture. Communities, as a consequence, differ with regard to their culture, civility, and relationships.

Peterson and Seligman[10] cited six core virtues for individuals and citizens of character that can also apply to entire communities. These include:

- Courage: exercising will in the face of external and internal opposition in order to accomplish goals. Bravery, persistence, and integrity are needed.
- Justice: civic strengths that include citizenship, social responsibility, and leadership to get things accomplished ethically and fairly.
- Humanity: interpersonal displays of kindness, care and love, and social intelligence and awareness of the motives and feelings of others.
- Temperance: humility and modesty, self-regulation and self-control, as well as prudence and forgiveness.
- Transcendence: forging connections through demonstrating appreciation, gratitude, hope, optimism, humor, and a sense of purpose.
- Wisdom: cognitive strengths, creativity, open-mindedness, judgment, critical thinking, perspective, and love of learning.

Communities and citizens need these virtues to work together because they are vital in developing a focus on the common good.

ISSUES AND THE COMMON GOOD

The concept of the common good presents challenges, particularly for a society that desires instant gratification. Immediate results do not come easy, and in some cases the benefits may be hard to calibrate. In addition, all political, corporate, and special interest proposals are couched in terms of enhancing the common good, regardless of whether they actually do. Conflict exists at times in what is in the interest of the common good versus personal self-interest.

American society is diverse and pluralistic: not everyone will agree on matters concerning the commonweal and their impact on individuals. People disagree as to what the common good is. Programs cost money, require sacrifice, and results are not always immediate or guaranteed. In addition, long-term support is difficult as priorities vary. Different people have different expectations and opinions of the "good life."

At times self-interest is dressed in the cloak of virtue and public welfare. There is another side to the relationship of the common good and individual self-interest. In some cases, enhancing and protecting the common good can threaten individual rights. A prime example is programs aimed at enhancing the security of the people, communities, and the nation as a whole, which can restrict individual opportunities, privacy, and choices.

Divergent perspectives about what constitutes the common good exist in a pluralistic society. Communities can be repressive: exploitive cultural, social, or political structures can diminish the rights of individuals and the common good. Suppression can come from either the political left or the political right. Both have tendencies that can compromise individual rights and freedom. For example, both liberals and conservatives have challenged freedom of speech in the past. What is offensive to one may not be to the other.

THE GOOD SOCIETY

Healthy dialogue and trust are essential for a good society, even if some find the debate offensive. People and societies that commit to values and principles can overcome fragmentation and stand firm against undemocratic schemes and practices. Commitment to shared values is a powerful coalescing force that builds relationships and mutual encouragement. The power of ideas, values, and principles enhances the community's ability to not only survive but also flourish through commitment, trusting relationships, and social and internal controls because people want to do the right thing.

Amitai Etzioni states, "A good society . . . fosters trust among its members not solely or even primarily to enhance their trust in the government but to cultivate a better society, one in which certain types of conduct are preferred over others by the community, rather than leaving it to each individual to judge what is 'good behavior.'"[11] In addition to trust, Etzioni indicates that in a good society there is a moral dimension that cultivates stewardship beyond individual preferences and interests.

Individuals as citizens have a "moral voice"[12] that they need to use to speak out and make choices to ensure decisions are in harmony with ideals and principles. Communities and politics have an external voice that is present in political and other decisions. Public relations, the press, and officials use that voice to coax, sway, censure, and control the public.

Moral dialogue requires a "robust public dialogue"[13] in which differences and similarities are discussed, explored, and engaged openly, even if it does not bring agreement. These dialogues are not easy, particularly in a contemptuous climate and society. However, if they are held, they can lead to the clarification and interpretation of values through analysis and understanding. A shared understanding can be achieved and the possibility of shared consensus attained, but civility is necessary and essential.

Questions of service and sacrifice are raised. Questions of rightness are challenged. Issues of virtue promote debate of interpretation, application, and legitimacy of values and positions. A serious question is: When conflicts such as these occur, what is the recourse? And how do we engage to address that possible conflict?

These dialogues can take place through person-to-person meetings, via regional or national networking, in the media, within organizations and associations, and even in political discussions (not to be confused with the vacuous so-called presidential debates). Agreement may not be achieved, but openness and clarification can be attained, along with clarification of values and their application.

All of this raises the concept of the role of citizens as members of communities and society. According to Peter Block,[14] citizenship is a state of being that involves acting and care. Citizens hold themselves accountable for the well-being of others, use their power and take action, and don't defer their power to others. In this, citizens have integrity and a moral duty. Working collectively with others helps restore the greater community. Citizens have choices and must accept accountability.

In a democracy, active participation of citizens in politics and civic life is paramount. If the government is to serve the people, then the people must become involved and abide by the rules and obligations they have as citizens, including the ability to dissent and criticize the government.

While citizenship requires participation, it also calls for patience and civility. In that regard, citizens must invest time and hard work to engage in constant vigilance of social and political issues. Citizens must be active, not passive, ensuring that government officials treat citizens with equal dignity and respect.

Shared values direct relationships and encourage a civil society. They bind us together despite our diverse backgrounds into a society and culture of mutual connection as we pursue our individual purpose in life.

WHAT CITIZENS MUST KNOW

- Personal, social, political, or economic change can bring about conflict socially, organizationally, or individually.
- The commons have been historically a meeting place for the entire community: a symbol of a shared life and interests. The commonweal concerns the welfare of the community—the common good.
- Aristotle and Rousseau expressed the common good as general will over the "rulers good."
- Leadership and active citizenship are necessary for considering and proposing actions based on the common good—the greater good, not self-interest.

- Citizens must move from simplistic binary thought to reason and reflection to understand the complexities of values, rights, and justice.
- The commonweal and common good are based on values and principles that are unifying forces. Society has centripetal and centrifugal forces.
- Citizens must have a moral voice in considering, analyzing, and evaluating political and other proposals.
- A commitment to the common good requires greater demands on some citizens than others because of economics, circumstances, or ability.
- A civil society is a commitment to values and principles that bind people together in an atmosphere open to discussion, debate, and dialogue.

NOTES

1. Christopher R. Mitchell, "Conflict, Social Change and Conflict Resolution. An Enquiry," Berghof Research Center for Constructive Conflict Management, https://www.berghof-foundation.org/fileadmin/redaktion/Publications/Handbook/Dialogue_Chapters/dialogue5_mitchell_lead-1.pdf.

2. Mitchell, "Conflict, Social Change and Conflict Resolution."

3. George A. Goens, *It's Not My Fault: Victim Mentality and Becoming Response-able* (Lanham, MD: Rowman & Littlefield, 2017), 17.

4. John Haidt, "The Age of Outrage," speech to the Manhattan Institute, November 15, 2017, https://www.manhattan-institute.org/html/2017-wriston-lecture-age-outrage-10779.html.

5. Manuel Velasquez, Claire Andre, Thomas Shanks, and Michael J. Meyer, "The Common Good," *Issues in Ethics* (Spring 1992), http://scu.edu/ethics.resources/ethical-decision-making/the-common-good/.

6. Sharon Daloz Parks, "How Then Shall We Live?" in *Living the Questions: Essays Inspired by the Work and Life of Parker J. Palmer*, ed. Sam M. Intrator (San Francisco: Jossey-Bass, 2005).

7. Barbara Crosby and John Bryson, *Leadership for the Common Good* (New York: John Wiley and Sons, 2005), 360.

8. James McGregor Burns, *Leadership* (New York: Harper Torchbooks, 1978), 89–90.

9. Burns, *Leadership*, 460.

10. Christopher Peterson and Martin E. P. Seligman, *Character Strengths and Virtues* (New York: Oxford University Press, 2004), 29–30.

11. Amitai Etzioni, *The Common Good* (Hoboken, NJ: Wiley, 2014), 150.

12. Etzioni, *The Common Good*, 152.

13. Sam McLean, "Politics of the Comment Good" (October 2009), http://
www.thersa.org/discover/publications-and-articles/rsa-blogs/2009/10/politics-
of-the-common-good.

14. Peter Block, *Community: The Structure of Belonging* (San Francisco, CA:
Barrett-Koehler, 2009), 65.

4

A CIVIL SOCIETY

Nothing is more wonderful than the art of being free, but nothing is harder to learn how to use that freedom.

—Alexis de Tocqueville

Many people across the globe live under autocracies, dictatorships, monarchies, and other forms of corrupt and stultifying regimes. Totalitarian governments place one major expectation on their citizens—compliant and submissive conformity. Discussion and debate are not tolerated and, in fact, punished. These governments prefer and demand apathetic citizens who yield to authority.

Citizenship in a democratic republic, however, comes with expectations and commitments: to keep and maintain democracy. This is no small task. If citizens do not meet them, fractures begin, and public policy falls into the hands of a few power interests. Detachment and self-absorption can be a slow-growing cancer with severe consequences.

Margaret Thatcher delivered a lecture at the Hillsdale Center for Constructive Alternatives, in which she stated:

Sir Edward Gibbon (1737–1794), author of *The Decline and Fall of the Roman Empire*, wrote tellingly of the collapse of Athens, which was the birthplace of democracy. He judged that, in the end, more than they wanted freedom, the Athenians wanted security. Yet they lost everything—security, comfort, and freedom. This was because they wanted not to give to society, but for society to give to them. The

freedom they were seeking was freedom *from* responsibility. It is no
wonder, then, that they ceased to be free.[1]

Maintaining a democratic republic is demanding and requires dedication. When Benjamin Franklin was asked at the close of the Constitutional Convention whether the outcome was a monarchy or a republic, Franklin infamously stated, "A republic, if you can keep it."

America at the time was a true experiment: a country formulated on
values, not royalty or autocracy. The Declaration of Independence cites
"unalienable rights" as life, liberty, and the pursuit of happiness, in addition to proclaiming that all men "are created equal." Values bind the
United States and local communities together. They formulate a shared
vision for the country and also require citizen involvement in community
and political affairs.

America was founded on extremely important values that raise critical
questions and the moral imperative behind them. Keeping the flame of
democracy alive requires active, not deferential, efforts and commitment
to ideals. In fact, as history demonstrates, people are willing to die for
values because they are at the core of a meaningful life and contiguous
progress.

Republics have four basic qualities: popular sovereignty, a sense of
the common good, civic virtue demonstrated by citizens, and a resistance
to the forces of corruption.[2] Popular sovereignty simply means that political power rests in the hands of the people, not power groups, families,
corporations, or oligarchs.

Civic virtue involves citizens dedicated to their duties to maintain
their rights and the country's integrity to its principles. Civic virtue and
civility are related because when civility is lacking, civic virtue is lost.

Corruption, the fourth concern, is evident today as it has been in the
past. When special or personal favoritism is placed above the general will
and the common good, then corruption exists. Political power in the
hands of a few corrupts and results in lost faith and credibility in politics
and government. As a result, support for government and society dissi-
pates, and democracy is weakened and threatened. Without active attention and involvement by citizens, complacency leads to the erosion of
confidence and hope.

Citizens must believe government is honest to actively commit and
participate. If the cards are stacked, citizens will not engage. Voices

cannot or will not be heard, and intelligent individuals will not run for office. The old adage, "bad money drives out good money," applies here. Corrupt government and politicians drive out good candidates. A political class, powerful political families on both sides of the aisle, and self-interest-driven politics circumvent the common good and a civil society.

Citizens must learn and understand that discussion and proposals from a variety of perspectives are an important part of living in a democracy. Debate and contrary opinions are necessary if a democratic society is to remain free. Free speech is vital. The temptation to cut people off who have a different view or perspective is dangerous and despotic. The base of democracy is citizen action and tolerance for divergent and conflicting viewpoints. Dealing with them civilly is a major responsibility, but not always easy.

CIVILITY

P. M. Forti stated, "Civility means a great deal more than just being nice to one another. It is complex and encompasses learning how to connect successfully and live with others, developing thoughtfulness, and fostering effective self-expression and communication. Civility includes courtesy, politeness, mutual respect, fairness, good manners."[3]

Civil behavior involves respect and restraint so people are able to communicate and speak freely and share their stories and perspectives. Civility does not mean agreement, but it does require deference to the principles of character and courtesy—and democracy.

Civility is perceived to be a problem in the United States today. Research done each year since 2010 by KRC Research indicate that America has a major civility problem.

> In this latest installment, we find Americans continuing to report a severe civility deficit in our nation, one that shows no signs of letting up. The belief that the U.S. has a major incivility problem has even reached a record high (69%). Three quarters of Americans believe that incivility has risen to crisis levels, a rate that has significantly increased since January 2016. The same proportion feels that the U.S. is losing stature as a civil nation (73%). These statistics, consistently high year after year, are a sobering commentary on the state of civility in our country.[4]

The study found that 84 percent of the respondents reported having experienced incivility: 25 percent reported incivility online, compared to "a mere 9%" in 2011. Concerning the future, 56 percent of those in the study believe civility will get worse.

Those responsible for incivility, as identified by respondents, included politicians (75 percent), internet/social media (69 percent), news media (59 percent), America's youth (45 percent), and demonstrators/protesters (44 percent). Concerning politics, 79 percent describe the 2016 presidential election as uncivil.

Despite the perception of incivility, Americans do not take personal responsibility for it, nor do they perceive their associates as uncivil. Some 94 percent indicated that they are always or usually civil, followed by people they know (78 percent), people with whom they work (73 percent), and people in their communities (57 percent).

They believe (54 percent) that incivility deters people from going into public service. In addition, the consequences of incivility include harassment and intimidation and threats (89 percent), violent behavior (88 percent), online bullying/cyberbullying (87 percent), and discrimination against people (88 percent).

As a result of incivility, participants recommend the following changes in their lives:

- 59 percent stop paying attention to political conversations and debates
- 56 percent defend or speak on behalf of people or groups they thought were treated uncivilly
- 53 percent stop doing business with a company because someone from that enterprise was uncivil to them

The poll also asked respondents to identify what actions should be taken to curb incivility. Social media was identified as an issue, with 58 percent of respondents indicating that media sites and search engines should eliminate "fake" news posts and articles. Almost half (49 percent) specified that civility training should occur in schools and colleges, 40 percent felt that employers should encourage employees to report incivility at work, and 30 percent indicated that employers should be held responsible for eliminating incivility at work.

Individuals (75 percent) in the study reported that they are willing to set a good example and are willing to examine their own behavior. All organizations should review and evaluate their workplaces and act to correct deficiencies.

The study recognized political polarization as an obstacle in finding common ground. "The political polarization in America that has only become worse applies to civility as well. Whereas some people think that our public squares are better because citizens say whatever is on their minds, others believe our public squares have become breeding places for hate and lies. If Americans could become more accepting of arguments on both sides of the political spectrum and listen more to each other, common ground could be rediscovered and our civility crisis eased."[5]

INCIVILITY

Disagreement and opposition are common because freedom of speech guarantees that differing issues and opinions surface. The expectation of citizen engagement and the power of the electorate inevitably raise differences in philosophy and contrary interpretations and solutions.

Living democratic values, however, is not conflict-free because freedom creates debate and discussion. However, that does not entail name-calling, disrespect, isolating, shouting down, hovering in "safe spaces," blaming, or labeling people into despicable categories.

Good manners, tolerance, and personal responsibility seem to be forgotten. Children observe adults being rude, insulting, and brash. Society seems harsher and divisive. Rancor and recklessness are evident in politics and social media, as well as in everyday life. Disrespectful actions are displayed in all contexts, including the halls of Congress.

Refusal to acknowledge the presence of individuals when they are physically present is an uncivil act and demonstrates a lack of respect. The message is "the person does not matter." Indifference is contrary to human dignity. A seemingly nonaggressive behavior, like ignoring the presence, no less the comments, of others is not civil behavior and purges any opportunity for discourse.

Elie Wiesel's poignant reminder that the opposite of love is not hate, "it is indifference," applies to communication in society. It can lead to dismissal, detachment, and lack of feeling toward others. In essence, indifference essentially places individuals in a less-than-equal category. Indifference creates serious issues, as individuals basically don't care and adopt gross apathy and disregard for others: often this situation causes people to retreat into a shell. That position jeopardizes democracy because there are times when citizens must become involved, speak out, and seek solutions in a common venture with others of contrary views or status.

The term *incivility* has Latin roots, according to the Oxford dictionary, meaning "not of a citizen"—*incivilis*. The responsibility of all citizens is to meet their civil duty with dignity and in tune with democratic principles. Incivility is contrary to those responsibilities.

Incivility opens the doors to bullying, name-calling, and stereotypes that segregate and demean people. It occurs in schools as children face bullying and stigmatizing that is derisive and hurtful, sometimes culminating in physical and psychological consequences. The pain of these circumstances can last a lifetime.

Incivility, according to Porath and Pearson,[6] also takes its toll in the workplace. Disrespect causes people to lose their jobs and become less creative, and work-life quality decreases. Relationships become damaged, and, in some cases, retaliation takes place, fostering even more acrimony. In schools, businesses, or society, these effects become alienating, causing cooperation and assistance to recede into darkness.

People who experience incivility can develop close bonds and a shared dislike toward those who were the culprits. Retaliation, sometimes silent and subtle, happens, inflicting damage on the perpetrators as well as infecting the attitudes and behavior of everyone else.

Simply witnessing incivility at work has negative consequences because performance declines and cooperation deteriorates, damaging the organizational culture. Individuals fear proposing ideas to solve problems and are apprehensive to participate actively for fear of retribution and sarcasm. In summary, performance quality decreases, commitment declines, and anxiety and frustration increase. In the workplace, some leave their jobs or spend less time at their work.

To maintain an effective and functioning free society, the following characteristics are essential[7]:

- Civic space for citizens to pursue what they believe is in their own and the public's interests

- Freedom of speech, written and spoken, which may include criticism of those in power
- Right of association and the exercise of collective action
- Citizen influence on public policies and programs, as well as on attitudes and behavior
- Effective and responsive government officials who perceive citizens as a starting point for public policy

Individual rights are requisite in a free society, and it is the fundamental duty of citizens to protect those rights. They must be willing to accommodate and guarantee the freedom of others to speak and exercise them as well. Certainly, this includes respectful behavior and conduct toward others. In essence, society provides protection, and in return citizens must treat others with dignity, respect, and compassion.

Civility is not a sign of weakness. Actually, it is a demanding concept requiring honest debate, listening to contrasting ideas, and having the strength to respect adversaries when ideas are challenging. It requires the maturity to engage others and understand ideas, values, or principles and to comprehend others' experiences and points of view philosophically and conceptually.

Insecure individuals, as well as those who lack knowledge, can easily fall into hostile and aggressive language, profanity, and physicality. The foundation of citizenship is respect for ideas and values and living and defending them, even if doing so means standing against the majority or the crowd.

Americans have rights in a democracy, including voting for the protection of life and property, the right to an education, an independent system of justice, freedom of the press, and a social safety net. In return, citizens have an obligation to[8]:

- Participate in government by voting, speaking out, and actively taking part in the process of governance to ensure the integrity of individual freedoms
- Build networks and informal structures that undergird local communities and democracy and participate, assuming responsibility
- Act with respect and compassion with others, even those with whom there are disagreements
- Obey the law

- Participate in causes that promote the common good
- Be willing to defend the country

Obviously, citizens must engage in national and local conversations about issues. Waiting for others to take the initiative and standing silent is not what the founders of this country believe was sufficient to "keep" the republic. Self-government depends on citizens using their ability to speak out and assembling to express themselves and establish priorities and solutions.

CIVIC VIRTUE AND COMMUNITIES

When people look to buy a home, they want a neighborhood and good neighbors. Politeness, kindness, and courtesy are important. These qualities also create a positive corporate or business culture.

By uniting with others in common purpose, social capital increases, which simply means enhancing the capacity of people to work together across boundaries. Instead of pitting one group against another, people learn together and develop new understandings. A sense of inclusiveness develops, along with productive reciprocity.

By doing so, mobilized citizens share responsibility and inspire each other to connect and work as a moral duty to ensure the common good and the welfare of others. Engaging different perspectives and voices can bring people together to find common purpose and create a sense of trust in the process.

American society requires leadership at every level. Local neighborhoods and communities need value-based leadership if progress is to be made on issues and problems. Expecting government officials to provide leadership is not sufficient to meet civic responsibilities—leadership by citizens is required at all levels of society and in all communities.

John Gardner stated, "We must develop networks of leaders who accept some measure of responsibility for the society's shared concerns. Call them networks of responsibility, leaders of disparate or conflicting interests who undertake to act together on behalf of the shared concerns of the community or nation."[9] Finding common ground to ensure integrity to principles is difficult but critical if citizens and others are to act with honor and distinction.

A civil society must exist for freedom to endure. Democracy depends on being able to raise issues and engage in rational and civil discourse. If free speech and civility are diminished, then society and other freedoms are jeopardized. Silence is not a virtue when liberty and equality are threatened. Civility creates a safe platform for dialogue and discussion and can build understanding and connection.

Political campaigns bring coarseness and occasional rants, along with vulgarity toward policies and candidates. Sometimes the incivility of an individual's preferred candidate is overlooked while the incivility of the other is reviled. Unfortunately, incivility and scandals get more attention than the substance of policies and proposals and present obstacles to citizen attention and understanding of issues and concerns.

POLITICS AND CIVILITY

Civility and politics seem like an oxymoron today. While the word *civility* is used in the contemporary political environment, its practice becomes a victim of narcissism, propaganda, and marketing. The ultimate goal is to gain financing and political power.

Individuality is a part of society, but commitment to the community is also an important foundation. Civic obligations are not really an option: they are not a matter of choice, and, as Gibbons stated about Rome, freedom from responsibility can lead to no freedom at all.

Former senator Bill Bradley stated, "The government is not irrelevant. It must be the force that sets the standards, establishes the policies, and helps with resources and with defining the common good."[10] He indicated that getting government to act for the common good is placed in the hands of citizens who must not shy away from discourse and action that is required for sustaining a democracy.

Bradley believes in the optimism of Americans to overcome difficulty and improve conditions—all part of the country's heritage and spirit: "Optimism is one of our great virtues. No circumstance is beyond improvement. No predicament is hopeless. In an age where change is the rule, our nation, which was born out of change and remains dedicated to its healthy cultivation, will not only survive but prosper. As Robert Frost wrote, we have promises to keep, and miles to go before we sleep."[11]

To keep those promises, the political process must be civil. Otherwise, there will be no understanding of diverse viewpoints. Talking past each other is not discourse. Derision is not a strategy for success.

Citizens have to be aware that narrow political interests can be cancerous to the common good and feed incivility because some politicians become indifferent to those who cannot contribute to their political largesse. The development of strong connections between congressman and senators and lobbying networks, complete with their fundraising, works on behalf of special interests. Power is the destination, and money is the vehicle.

Political campaigns revolve around money and, correspondingly, require that, if elected, officials do what the cash suppliers desire and need. Without money, buying media time and getting exposure are difficult. Once elected, congressional representatives spend exorbitant time making calls soliciting funds for future elections. The result is "a permanent political class increasingly remote from everyday Americans and a system that could lead to the ultimate destruction of the republican ideal."[12]

If self- and special interest replaces the common good and the notion of a civil society, then a republic will not stand. Abandoning historical values and institutions compromise American ideals, and a closed political system will expand and prevail. At the core of the United States are principles and values that, if lost, will render America rootless.

A civil society has the means to guard against power flowing from the hands of a few. The tools of free speech, which must remain open, and fulfilling the collective duties and responsibilities of citizens are really marks of our national character. Vaclav Havel said, "Talk about civil society is, of course, talk about the character of the state."[13]

A civil society and active citizenry can stop the growth of conditions that fester and have a problematic impact on society. Politicians and officials should encourage, awaken, and strengthen the values that are at the heart of democracy in order to serve their constituents and the common good.

WHAT CITIZENS MUST DO

- Become actively involved in political and community affairs and meet their citizenship responsibilities.

- Learn and understand the depth of the core values of American democracy.
- Comprehend the essence of individual rights and the importance of understanding their relationship to the common good.
- Be civil to those in personal, political, and social spheres.
- Understand and defend the concepts of a free society and maintain them particularly in times of controversy and dissent.
- Provide leadership—formal and informal—in communities and the nation to address issues and find resolution to them.
- Actively work for candidates to ensure that the common good, not personal gain and special interests, is addressed and corruption is averted.
- Stand up and speak to the moral imperative necessary and required to support freedom and equality.
- Vote for candidates with reasoned desire to find solutions and defeat those who serve special interests.

NOTES

1. Margaret Thatcher, "The Moral Foundations of Society," *Imprimis* 24, no. 3.

2. Gary Hart, *The Republic of Conscience* (New York: Blue Writer Press, 2015), 1–2.

3. Tina Katsanos, Vaughn Schmutz, Kendra Jason, Michelle Pass, and Honore Missihoun, "Promoting Civility and Professionalism in the Classroom," http://journal.uncc.edu/facultyguide/article/view/381/375/page2.

4. "Civility in America VII: The State of Civility," Weber, Shandwick and PowellTate, KRC Research, http://www.webershandwick.comuploads/news/files/civility_in_america_the_state_of_civility.pdf, 2–22.

5. "Civility in America VII," 22.

6. Christine Porath and Christine Pearson, "The Price of Incivility," *Harvard Business Review* (January–February 2013), R13013.

7. Brian O'Connell, *Civil Society: The Underpinnings of American Democracy* (Lebanon, NH: University Press of New England, 1999), 4.

8. O'Connell, *Civil Society*, 12.

9. Ed O'Malley and David Chrislip, *For the Common Good: Redefining Civic Leadership* (Wichita: Kansas Leadership Center, 2013).

10. Bill Bradley, *Time Present, Time Past* (New York: Alfred A. Knopf, 1996), 414.

11. Bradley, *Time Present, Time Past*, 415.

12. Hart, *The Republic of Conscience*, xix.

13. Vaclav Havel, *The Art of the Impossible: Politics as Morality in Practice* (New York: Alfred A. Knopf, 1997), 148.

5

THE BEDROCK OF DEMOCRACY
Public Education

Preach, my dear Sir, a crusade against ignorance; establish & improve the law for educating the common people. Let our countrymen know that the people alone can protect us against these evils, and that the tax which will be paid for this purpose is not more than the thousandth part of what will be paid to kings, priests & nobles who will rise up among us if we leave the people in ignorance.
—Thomas Jefferson, letter to George Wythe, 1786

Thomas Jefferson, Samuel Adams, Benjamin Franklin, John Adams, and others promoted the imperative of an educated electorate to engage in self-government. They believed that a republic could exist and survive only if citizens were educated well enough to comprehend issues, express themselves, and participate actively in self-government.

Education, not indoctrination, was the goal and became the bedrock for the maintenance and resilience of society and government. Adlai Stevenson, former presidential candidate in the 1950s, stated, "The free common school system is the most American thing about America."[1]

Public education is a common good and basic right necessary for active involvement in American democracy. It prepares citizens to sustain democracy. Generally, Americans do not consider democracy to be threatened, and some take it for granted, not understanding that it requires an ongoing, conscious effort. "Perhaps the biggest threat to democracy and our times is complacency. If we consider democracy as a given, we

are unlikely to engage in the sustained efforts needed to bring it to frui-
tion."[2]

A republic requires citizens to stay informed, to participate in public
discussion, to attend meetings, and to vote. Acquiescence and submission
to circumstances are not acceptable. Susan B. Anthony, in a letter to a
friend in 1900, clearly supported education for all when she stated, "A
Republican government should be based on free and equal education
among the people."[3]

Schools play a critical role in helping students understand the obligations and attitudes of citizenship: critical thinking, researching, accessing
and evaluating information, and determining the truthfulness and accuracy of analyses and claims.[4]

Citizens must be active participants in community affairs and contribute and strengthen the nation economically and culturally by increasing
their knowledge and by being creative and fulfilling their own potential.
Strong character and endurance are necessary to confront life with its
challenges and defining moments. It also demands standing up for principle at times when it may not be popular.

Public education in this sense was to teach the core of common values:
"pure republican principles and practices that united Americans"[5] based
on the values exemplified in the Declaration of Independence and the
Constitution. Education prepares individuals to make wise choices as
citizens, as well as personally.

RIGHTS AND DUTIES

Democracy stands on specific values, which are the unifying foundation
for a civil society. Today, as in the past, civil rights concern the right to
be free from unequal treatment based on certain characteristics—race,
gender, and disability. Those rights protect against discrimination.

Civil liberties, however, are basic guaranteed rights and freedoms designated in the Bill of Rights, the Constitution, case law, and other legislation. Citizens have the freedom to pursue life, liberty, and happiness, but
these rights come with a price—the fulfillment of citizen responsibilities
and duties.

A duty has legal consequences. A responsibility is something citizens
should do but are not required by law to do. Voting is a responsibility

under this definition, as well as remaining informed of the issues affecting their communities and nation, respecting the rights, beliefs, and opinions of others, and participating in their local community.

Theodore Roosevelt stated, "It ought to be axiomatic in this country that every man must devote a reasonable share of his time to doing his duty in the political life of the community. No man has the right to shirk his political duties under whatever plea of pleasures or business."[6] Roosevelt declared, "The first duty of an American citizen, then, is that he shall work in politics; his second duty is that he shall do that work in a practical manner; and his third is that it shall be done in accord with the highest principles of honor and justice."

The terms *honor* and *justice* seem incongruous with the term *politics* in this day. Public officials elected by citizens through the ballot were to honor that selection by living and meeting standards of fidelity and integrity in serving the public and upholding the nation's principles. *Serve* is a key word: it concerns behavior and standing that meet the needs of the people with integrity and dignity.

Active participation in politics and government decision making is expected of citizens, but Roosevelt also stated that the work of a citizen has complexities and is not always easy. He cautioned that citizens must apply reason and should "neither be timid pessimists nor foolish optimists." Reason is essential in civil debate and discussions.

In more specific terms, Americans' legal duties include the following:

- Citizens must obey all local, state, and federal laws. Citizens have legal protection through laws, and they must accept and follow them.
- Jury duty is compulsory and is associated with individuals' right to a trial by a jury of one's peers.
- All minors must attend school, which is essential for the development of an educated citizenry.
- Paying taxes is the price for state and federal services and protections.
- At times, citizens must protect and defend the nation.

Sometimes individuals perceive citizenship as simply a means to provide for themselves. However, citizenship requires them to act and ensure they provide for democracy and a vibrant society and citizenry.

BRIEF HISTORY OF EDUCATION AND RIGHTS

Without education, the blemishes and darkness of some aspects of American history would not have been addressed and rectified. Education and commitment to core values were and remain vital to create and maintain an enlightened society.

Education strengthens American governance, politics, and culture. Schooling and education policy have been at the forefront of providing children with the knowledge, skills, and values necessary to succeed without regard to race, gender, or national origin.

In 1883, Frederick Douglass, in a speech at the National Convention of Colored Men, stated, "The fact remains that the whole country is directly interested in the education of every child that lives within its borders. The ignorance of any part of the American people so deeply concerns all the rest that there can be no doubt of the right to pass laws compelling the attendance of every child at school."[7]

This premise has been pursued significantly throughout American history. Schooling and education became more systematic after the American Revolution. There was some sense of urgency to ensure that citizens would understand public issues and select leaders who would sustain liberty and order in a new political system. Very basically, people had to learn to read and write to be an active and effective citizen.

In 1785, the Land Ordinance was passed, which included the stipulation for funding public education. The Northwest Ordinance of 1787 established governance for the Northwest Territory, promoted a public university, and instituted natural rights for the area, complete with the prohibition of slavery. The goal of education was to ensure that citizens knew their rights and could contribute to their own political welfare.

Horace Mann, in 1837, proposed a "common school" where students would learn a common body of knowledge and democratic values so that knowledge is applied and not corrupted. He was a leader of the education reform movement to create a universal standard education in Massachusetts and to eliminate regional and communal differences.

In 1862, the Morrill Act created land-grant colleges to teach content related to agriculture and mechanical arts, as well as other scientific and classical studies. Eligible states received land for establishing these institutions.

School reform centered on equality in the twentieth century. With industrial expansion and the influx of immigrants, schools provided education to low-income children to help them with employment and social mobility. Immigrants received an education that assisted them to assimilate and to contribute to society, as well as achieve their own aspirations.

The 1900s also emphasized vocational education. Some individuals thought that the general curriculum was too academic, and experts suggested a vocational track with occupational programs for those children expected to work in factories, in commercial enterprises, or as housewives. After World War II, the GI Bill of Rights opened doors for veterans and was a preeminent program to help them develop the ability and capability not only to fulfill themselves and their families but also to increase the economic posture of the United States.

In the 1950s "separate but equal" schools were challenged, and *Brown vs. Board of Education* in 1954 was a landmark case rejecting the constitutionality of school segregation. In the 1970s, Title IX was passed eliminating discrimination on the basis of gender in any federally funded education program or activity. Openness to all citizens became a greater reality, unlocking doors previously shut and discordant with the principle of equality.

In 1973, Section 504 of the Rehabilitation Act guaranteed certain rights to people with disabilities. Children with disabilities could not be denied participation or be the subject of discrimination in any program or activity funded by an executive agency. The Individuals with Disabilities Act 2004 ensured that children with disabilities will be provided with a free and appropriate public education.

Over time, schools became more inclusive and in harmony with the stated values of the founding documents. The essential purpose from the founders' point of view was to support the education of citizens so they are well versed in their rights and responsibilities, as well as the skills and intelligence necessary to sustain the nation's governance, society, and culture.

Democracy is a way of life—both ideally and pragmatically. Living together in community requires understanding democratic principles based on the belief that people can rule themselves, work through conflict, coalesce around common values, and elect representatives and hold them accountable.

Public education has evolved since its inception, facing dramatic societal and economic changes, social and political crises, and foreign and domestic conflict. How well has public education done in facing these circumstances?

The United States has become the most prominent country in the world due in part to the ability, creativity, and endurance of citizens, the vast majority of whom have been educated in public schools. American education provided for the advancement of citizens individually and collectively. Employers have had citizens with appropriate education and training even through the shift from an agrarian to an industrial to a technological economy over the past 150 years.

A civil society rests on commitment, equality, freedom, and self-government, as well as the concepts of social and economic mobility, individual merit, and respect for others and the law. Without a firm basis in values and principles, society will fragment and disunite into chaos.

CHALLENGES TO EDUCATION

Sputnik and the rise of Russian space exploits in the late 1950s challenged the quality of American education, which then became a focal point for analysis and evaluation with specific emphasis on the sciences. In the 1980s, *A Nation at Risk* questioned the quality of public education outcomes, bringing with it local, state, and federal reforms. Out of the "At Risk" report came recommendations on content, time, teachers, standards, and governmental support.

Critics of public schools used test scores as the metric for determining their success. Test scores became the marker for success, along with other metrics—all products of quantitative business management. Ravitch indicated, "Because federal policies value only test scores, they have unleashed an almost fanatical obsession with data based on test scores."[8] The assumption is that reality can be defined through numbers and statistics.

In my previous book *The Fog of Reform*, I stated, "Public education has suffered from the tyranny of the tangible. The penchant to judge schools and teachers on the basis of test scores, graduation rates, suspension rates, or other metrics has run wild. In the debate about public schools, it basically boils down to 'if you can't measure it, it doesn't matter.' Schools appear to be successful if they get the numbers."[9]

In the process, other noble goals have dropped out of sight. Social studies, government, and philosophy courses are not considered essential in many schools. The fact of the matter is that competent citizens require much more than simply math, science, engineering, and technology.

Narrowing curriculum and reducing a focus on liberal arts create philosophical and ethical hazards for citizens and the country. Liberal arts prepare people to deal with complexity, diversity, and change, as well as provide broad content knowledge and higher-order thinking skills. Students learn to see beyond one perspective and encourage understanding even if they don't agree.

Education exists for societal and civic reasons beyond simply narrow employment and economic considerations. With universal education and the achievements for equal opportunity, education actually provides more and includes objectives like creativity, philosophy, character, and wisdom that cannot be reduced to a simple metric.

Understanding American culture, complete with its values, is necessary for all citizens in order to participate civilly, politically, and socially. Unifying a diverse nation, particularly in an era of identity politics, is not easy, but it remains one of the main challenges of education. The hope is that if people share a common education and understand core values, they will communicate and interact with each other civilly.

"Today, the mission of promoting cultural unity is more crucial than ever. The U.S. population has become more ethnically and linguistically diverse at the same time the economy has become more international. And in a world torn with ethnic strife, the ability to understand other perspectives and deal with conflict are critical skills."[10]

The debate in the past decades has been about the education that children should receive in terms of content and approach. John Dewey commented on a course of study of common learning and goals for community and democracy: "Men live in a community in virtue of the things which they have in common; and communication is the way in which they come to process things in common. What they must have in common are aims, beliefs, aspirations, knowledge—a common understanding."[11]

The vast majority of Americans agree with the unifying goals of public schools: access to free education, equal opportunity, and self-government. The general public basically recognizes the importance of helping children to be self-sufficient economically and socially, as well as supporting positive social conditions.

General agreement exists about the need for education in a democracy, but the "devil is in the details." Education requires deep thought and understanding: defining the meaning of the concepts of democracy, republicanism, civility, and freedom take work and discussion.

The conflict between individualism and communitarianism is always present: when individual ambitions and rights collide with social and community norms and needs: in other words, the conflict of individual good versus the common good. The fear of uniformity is the basis for challenging mandated programs and ideas.

The story and mythology of Americans is one of individualism and "can-do" spirit based on a self-reliant character. Hard work, generosity, and inventiveness are terms used to describe Americans, along with commitment and grit to succeed personally but also to overcome adversity, individually and nationally.

Critically, public schools taught values that promoted the common good and benefited society as a whole, the idea being that society is not to be fragmented into isolated individuals who are separate and apart from each other. Only as individuals participate as citizens in a local community can the common good and connections be achieved.

> For more than 250 years, Americans have shared a vision in which all citizens understand, appreciate, and actively engage in civic and political life—taking responsibility for building communities, contributing their diverse talents and energies to solve local and national problems, deliberating about public issues, influencing public policy, voting, and pursuing the common good. Americans know that it is a rare and precious gift to live in a society that permits and values such participation.[12]

Many people seek easy answers: simplicity in solution and ease of understanding and implementation. However, work is necessary. Time and reflection are required. And, certainly, reason and compassion are essential to a civil society.

WHAT CITIZENS MUST LEARN

- Education is important to the common good and an important aspect of the fabric of American life.
- People must understand the importance of public education to democracy and support it at the local, state, and federal levels.
- Individuals must be able to define their rights and duties as citizens and exercise them properly.
- People must understand that because of the principles under which the United States is formulated, American education has expanded and must be equally accessible to all segments of society.
- American education is challenged by the corporate sector and the lure of data management that can distract from the basic motivating principles under which education was proposed.
- People should realize civility is strengthened from an education that focuses on ideas, reason, and democratic values.

NOTES

1. Sarah Mondale and Sarah B. Patton, *School: The Story of American Public Education* (Boston: MA: Beacon Press, 2001), 1.

2. Kathy Hytten, "Democracy and Education in the United States," *Oxford Research Encyclopedia of Education*, March 2017, 8.

3. Center on Education Policy, "Why We Still Need Public Schools: Public Education for the Common Good," http://cep-dc.org.

4. Hytten, "Democracy and Education in the United States," 8.

5. Mondale and Patton, *School*, 5.

6. Theodore Roosevelt, "The Duties of American Citizenship," New York, January 26, 1883, http://gle.yale.edu/dutis-American-citizenship.

7. Frederick Douglass, "Speech, National Convention of Colored Men, Louisville, Kentucky, September 24, 1883," http://coloredconvention.org/items/show/554.

8. Diane Ravitch, *Reign of Error: The Hoax of the Privatization Movement and Danger to America's Public Schools* (New York: Knopf Doubleday, 2013).

9. George A. Goens, *The Fog of Reform* (Lanham, MD: Rowman & Littlefield, 2016), 8–9.

10. Center on Education Policy, "Why We Still Need Public Schools," 10.

11. E. D. Hirsch, *The Schools We Need and Why We Don't Have Them* (New York: Doubleday, 1996), 18.

12. Carnegie Corporation of New York and CIRCLE, *The Civic Mission of Schools* (New York: Carnegie Corporation and Center for Information and Research on Civic Learning and Engagement), 8.

6

EDUCATION, CIVILITY, AND DEMOCRACY

Where you see wrong or inequality or injustice, speak out, because this is your country. This is your democracy. Make it. Protect it. Pass it on.
—Thurgood Marshall

Man's capacity for justice makes democracy possible, but man's inclination to injustice makes democracy necessary.
—Reinhold Niebuhr

The United States offers its citizens two distinct but complementary promises. First, a country based on values that provides a national culture of freedom, equality, and self-government. Second, Americans have a unique opportunity to express their individualism to pursue "happiness" and to live a life of their choosing.

In a distinctive way, society is bound together by collaborative values, but with individuals being free to follow their bliss. Community and individualism together provide for self-government as well as self-determination. The balance of both is important, but there are concerns that America, at times, splinters because of individualistic self-interest. However, centralization and control dampens and handicaps the liberty, passion, and autonomy of individuals.

A civil society requires unity around core values, as well as security for people to exercise their freedoms in finding purpose and meaning. There are limits to society and government, as there are restrictions for individual's exercising their independence without regard to the rights of others. The collective rights enable individuals to be free, but they also require individuals to meet their responsibilities and duties to others and society.

A commitment to shared values is fundamental in a civil society because they are the foundation for making ethical decisions and developing a sense of collective and individual identity. Behavior is based on these values in the marketplace of life—neighborhoods, work, informal interactions, and others. They are invisible and unspoken ties that bind citizens together, which create a feeling of belonging. Communities and citizens need a sense of connection: the assumption is that this bond will continue into the future.

Citizenship requires a sense of interdependence to stand together for the good of the country and society. Tragedies or disasters that wreak havoc and endanger the welfare of the people or the stability of the nation make this apparent.

On the other side of the ledger, controversies and disputes can create alienation. But the answer lies not in fragmentation but in finding ways to come together, heal, and renew the commitment to civil ideals and values.

Liberty today is "held together not only by the principles of equality and freedom but also by the shared triumphs and tragedies of American life and by the experience of unity and diversity—of becoming one out of many not by denying our differences, but by rising above them when we are called."[1]

Individual growth and renewal are indispensable to communities and the country's resilience and regeneration. The community provides a safe harbor and a sense of connection and belonging from shared ideals. Mutual commitment beyond personal or materialistic desires nourishes the soul and character. Serving a larger "good," beyond self, is part of individual fulfillment.

Freedom requires a social commitment. As John Gardner stated, "As we enable the individual to enjoy greater freedom, we must at the same time provide him with opportunities for allegiance and commitment to goals larger than himself. Otherwise, freedom degenerates into sterile self-preoccupation. The most troublesome consequence of self-preoccupation is boredom, and the cure for boredom is not diversion: it is to find some work to do, something to care about."[2]

Gardner wrote those words at the end of the 1960s, one of the more tumultuous decades of national controversy, protests, and demonstrations. His words ring true today. National renewal requires a shared vision and commitment to collective values. He wrote, "We have in the tradition of this nation a well-tested framework of values: justice, liberty, equality of opportunity, the worth and dignity of the individual, brotherhood, individual responsibility. These are all supremely compatible with social renewal. Our problem is not to find better values but to be faithful to those we profess."[3]

DELIBERATION

Part of the social order requires confronting agreement as well as controversy. Amitai Etzioni asserts that deliberation and reflective thought are "the process whereby reasoned people exchange views and negotiate a new course."[4] Deliberation moves beyond superficiality to examining values of right versus wrong and ethical versus unethical. What are the overarching values at play? This reasoning process can include individuals but also groups.

In reasoned deliberation, individuals and groups are free to choose a course, which requires an understanding of values, the moral implications of options, and the legal authority and correctness of them. This is true whether dealing with personal or societal questions. Responsibilities and duties require moral and ethical considerations and a true understanding of both individual and social issues and their implications.

Ethical questions and dilemmas are a consistent part of life. An education provides students with exposure to dealing with them in the safe context of a classroom, through case studies and other means to ascertain the impact of various options and their short- and long-term implications. Engagement in these discussions concerns both content and values.

Making a case for a position and playing out the effects provides a concrete understanding of the ethical repercussions of judgments. The role of individuals, as well as greater society, also is highlighted to determine the consequences for single citizens as well as groups. Changes in the country came from a commitment to the nation's principles, through reasoned debate, thoughtful action, and enlightened mutual interest.

EDUCATION: PERSPECTIVES

All children have things in common: "their common humanity, their human rights and aspirations, and their futures to which they are destined as equal members of our society."[5] They all have the same rights and responsibilities as citizens, and they all should know and understand them. Their future and their course in life rest on the quality of an academic education and understanding the principles and concepts of a democratic society.

Education must balance education for citizenship and educating people to meet their individual ambitions. In actuality, maybe the balance is not that large, because both are interwoven and complementary. Should education be directed to ensure that all children need and receive the same content, or should the focus be based on individual interests and choices? These questions are not singular and independent: they actually define a cohesive educational approach.

The United States has been committed to the principle of equal educational opportunity. First, all children should have access to quality schools, excellent teachers, safe environments, quality facilities, and programs that provide the knowledge, skills, and values to enable them to follow their calling.

The second issue concerns the purpose and nature of the curricular and instructional program. Differences exist between the emphases of the curriculum: Is it to impart knowledge and understanding of the principles of American democracy and the skills and complex thinking to be a fully participating citizen?

Essentialists promote a designated core of knowledge—intellectual skills and moral standards—that all children must learn. Progressives, by contrast, endorse an educational focus on an individual child's desires and choices and how to learn rather than on a universal content.

The different approaches to education reflect an emphasis on community (collective goals as a nation) versus an emphasis on individuality (personal interests and desires). Both collective and individual needs are defined in American documents for societal cohesion around values and the contribution individuals can make by shaping their skills and perspectives and applying their creativity.

In actuality, virtue exists in both the "essentialist" and the "progressive" approaches. Students benefit from each, with greater emphasis on one than on the other at different ages or periods of their lives.

Children grow into an unknown and evolving future, and education provides the ballast for adapting to the times. It provides the groundwork and foundation to bring together a diverse population and prepare people for citizenship, as well as equip self-sufficient individuals to improve their lives and the condition of their communities.

E. D. Hirsch believes that children at the elementary level require a knowledge-specific education to become literate and independent people. Horace Mann, along with Thomas Jefferson, promoted the common school to provide "all children equally with the knowledge and skills to keep them economically independent and free."[6]

Since citizens live in a nation premised on ideas and values common to all, schools must provide instruction in those precepts so that they can learn, understand, and protect them. Without that understanding, they are unable to analyze and assess governmental or societal initiatives and motives affecting them. In a sense, an education protects citizens from a government that may not honorably or competently subscribe to the country's values and public interest and, in the process, suppress individuals' ability to pursue their aspirations.

A major impact on economic growth and a key to American competitiveness and prosperity is educated people. The term *intellectual capital* concerns the knowledge that makes one country more competitive and prosperous than others. Education is indispensable in developing and nurturing the leadership, entrepreneurship, and imagination that enlivens and supports the nation's economy and society. This substantiates the importance of ensuring that all children in all socioeconomic categories receive a quality education, not simply for themselves but also for the greater good of society.

Literacy is a fundamental goal of education nationally. Without literacy, segments of society will be dead-ended politically, economically, and socially. Communication cannot be done easily and effectively without an understanding of the common language. Being able to read and write has always been a priority of elementary school programs, and remains so today. Writing, in actuality, is thinking made visible. A clear connection exists between the capability of critical thinking and writing well. Without clear thinking, there will not be thoughtful written or verbal expression.

Universal education, according to Hirsch, includes "the coherent, cumulative core curriculum which instills consensus values such as civic duty, honesty, diligence, perseverance, respect, kindness, and independent-mindedness; which gives students step-by-step mastery of *procedural knowledge* in language arts and mathematics; which gives them step-by-step mastery of *content knowledge* in civics, science, the arts, and the humanities."[7] The essentialist position ensures a common and consistent education for all.

Progressives like John Dewey thought that early education did not have to be tied to specific content. The student, not content, was the focus as children actively experienced the world and were to be problem solvers and thinkers who raise questions and find meaning through experiences and exploration.

Student interests and questions spurred the study of content with emphasis placed on process and how individuals learn. The "what" is not specifically mandated: the focus is on "how" to learn—specifically, by experiencing freedom to learn and having public schools operate under democratic principles. Making education more relevant to the needs and interests of children is the goal.

Children in this situation learn to define problems, figure options to solve them, examine them in the light of previous experiences, and then test the best course of action. Active participation and experience are good teachers.

Progressive education, according to Alfie Kohn,[8] concerns:

- Attending to the whole child to become good learners and good people
- Learning with and from one another in a caring community
- Emphasizing collaborative problem-solving
- Emphasizing intrinsic motivation, not extrinsic reliance on grades or rewards
- Active learning is when students help design the curriculum, raise questions, and search for answers

Both essentialist and progressive education philosophies have merit. It is not to select one and reject the other. These two approaches confront both aspects of American government and society: the importance of education to understand the philosophical core and the values of the democracy, and also support individuality and the "pursuit of happiness" to meet independent needs and aspirations. Together these approaches provide a foundation for citizenship without pressing for conformity and indoctrination for governmental control of individual lives.

EDUCATION AND THE FUTURE

The future holds one certainty: change. Transformations are the consequence of artistry, inventiveness, and conflict. Preparing children for this life requires a comprehensive education so they can adapt to external conditions while finding personal satisfaction and joy in life.

An understanding across academic areas and principles and standards allows people to analyze and comprehend the possible implications of prospective change. Academics and values enable citizens to parse potential alterations and determine their integrity to civic and personal principles. In many cases there is nothing more practical.

Remember that a high school graduate of eighteen will, if they live an average lifespan, have more than sixty years of adult life to confront. During this time, renewal and adjustments are necessary. Having an ethical and normative framework for assessing transformations and evolutions and determining their ethical and moral integrity to core principles is necessary. Without that framework, appropriate judgments and decisions are difficult and can be precarious.

To put it in perspective, a teacher told his students, "My mother, who was born in 1910 and lived ninety years, saw the development of automobiles, radio and television, world wars, computers, air flight, technology, and the rise and fall of governments. In that lifetime she also saw a man land on the moon, something that for most of her life was science fiction." All children will encounter such dramatic events and experiences.

In pursuing their lives, each child must discover who they are—their beliefs, talents, passions, joys. Mindfulness about their relationship to others, to nature, and to themselves is necessary to live purposefully. Discovering strengths and passions and uniqueness and connections leads to their mission and purpose in life and, in this sense, how individuals contribute to the greater society.

Perceptions and creativity emerge if education is focused on opening minds and perspectives. "Being educated has three areas of emphasis. Educated people have the capacity to see with new eyes. Their minds are open and they perceive what is unfolding in the world and society with a fresh perspective. They are mindful and aware of the integration of issues and what is unfolding. Their minds are not closed to pursue and explore new ideas without filtering out new and innovative concepts."[9]

Education helps individuals have the capacity to sense and shape their futures and to think critically and discern the best course for a moral and good society. They must understand their responsibilities in a democracy and gain historical perspective about duties to their family, community, and country.

Values provide the lens through which integrity is determined and assessed. They also provide the foundation for skeptical or critical thinking, both of which are vitally important in a society in which social media, celebrities, and special interests tout slogans and propaganda, and politicians state issues and propose action.

"In essence, all children need a strong liberal arts education. Specialization and narrowness of their education is a disservice, not only to them, but also in the long term to our society. Problem solving involves a broad perspective across content, and a deep understanding of the principles and moral expectations to maintain and create a civil society."[10] Well-educated people master and revere knowledge and apply concepts and ethics to guide them personally and as citizens concerned with public policy.

SKILLS AND CONTENT

Basic skills are a prerequisite for more complex thinking. Adults must gather and organize information, define the values that support arguments, articulate ideas clearly, format new perspectives and ideas, and question and challenge assumptions and theories. The ability to analyze, synthesize, and evaluate issues and concepts are imperative for assuming the rights and responsibilities of American citizenship.

The intellectual skills of critical thinking and judgment about concerns, legislation, and candidates are important in making decisions that affect the future of the country and society. Reading critically, listening carefully, weighing evidence, and coming to thoughtful conclusions are necessary in today's society in determining the outcome of legislation or litigation.

The study of history is indispensable if individuals are to understand the past conflicts and decisions that worked to protect rights and freedoms. Understanding historical perspectives are necessary to "improve our imperfect democracy."[11] The study of civics, government, and economics provides understanding and perspective on issues and proposals. Students must be familiar with the content of the Constitution, the Bill of Rights, and the Declaration of Independence. How laws are made, the role of the Supreme Court, and major court decisions are areas that citizens need to understand.

In today's society, science and technological advances bring subtle and dramatic change and require understanding of science and mathematics. Grasping statistics, particularly how it pertains to public opinion polling, demographics, and data analysis, is necessary.

Today statistical data is used in scientific discussions, political opinions, marketing, and other forms of communication. In this regard, some basic statistical knowledge is essential to be able to discern the truth and not get fleeced by numbers, metrical data, or research designs. Citizens need the background to discern and question research design, data collection and analysis, and findings. Numbers appear to be objective, but they can be as inaccurate as the written word.

Some question the relevance of literature, works of fiction, and other literature. Through literature students learn about character, the human spirit and goodness, imagination, evil and moral issues, and other qualities of human nature. Children learn that people think differently and have contradictory points of view, as well as a unique life story.

Finally, the arts are not to be an extracurricular or cocurricular endeavor. They concern philosophy, creativity, social commentary, and imagination. In most totalitarian societies, the first groups persecuted or imprisoned are the creative artists of all types. Understanding cultural values and philosophical foundations are basic to comprehending and investigating principles, ethics, and morality.

Leon Botstein stated,

> The arts create and sustain new ways of keeping freedom from losing meaning. They help individuals retain their own sense of uniqueness in

a world in which the pressure to conform is intense. They fill out the hollow structures of democratic rights with meaning that is profoundly personalized. They provide the imaginative world in which each individual can find a place and effectively fight the battle against deadening conformity. They are not superfluous embellishments of life, the ornaments we can do without. Like science, making and appreciating of art is integral to the practice of freedom. The arts challenge the monopoly of commerce in matters of fundamental values. The many generations of philosophers who have pondered the integral relationship between beauty and truth, between aesthetics and ethics, have done so with extremely good reason. [12]

To create a civil society, a sense of community and personal awareness are necessary. To do so, citizens must be able to communicate well and speak and write from knowledge of principles and history in a respectable manner. Learning must continue after formal schooling ends. Understanding and growth should be a continuous aspect of each citizen's life.

WHAT CITIZENS MUST KNOW

- Society has two concepts that can work in harmony for the good of the country and individuals: national values and individualism.
- Education is geared to developing capable and conscientious citizens and for the pursuit of individual aspirations and growth.
- Shared values are fundamental to a civil society, which connects citizens to a sense of community and responsibility.
- Deliberation is a process of reason to exchange views and find a new course, which includes an understanding of values.
- Responsibilities and duties require moral and ethical considerations and behavior.
- All citizens need to understand the core principles and values that undergird American democracy.
- Both "essentialist" and "progressive" education agree that understanding civil behavior is essential to pursue individual interests and talents and meet the demands of citizenship.
- Literacy and thinking skills are elementary expectations for students.

- Education should help individuals discover themselves—talents and passions—as well as provide the ability to adapt to transforming times.
- A strong liberal arts education is important for all citizens to master knowledge, concepts, and understanding in academics, fine arts, and ethics and values.

NOTES

1. Yuval Levin, *The Fractured Republic: Renewing America's Social Contract in the Age of Individualism* (New York: Basic Books, 2017).

2. John W. Gardner, *The Recovery of Confidence* (New York: W. W. Norton, 1970), 77.

3. Gardner, *The Recovery of Confidence*, 131.

4. Amitai Etzioni, *The New Golden Rule* (New York: Basic Books, 1996), 97.

5. Mortimer J. Adler, *Paideia Problems and Possibilities* (New York: Macmillan, 1983), 5–6.

6. E. D. Hirsch, *The Schools We Need and Why We Don't Have Them* (New York: Doubleday, 1996), 17–18.

7. Hirsch, *The Schools We Need*, 236.

8. Alfie Kohn, "Progressive Education: Why It's Hard to Beat, But Also Hard to Find," http://www.alfiekohn.org/article/progressive-education/.

9. George A. Goens, *The Fog of Reform: Getting Back to a Place Called School* (Lanham, MD: Rowman & Littlefield, 2016), 62.

10. Goens, *The Fog of Reform*, 64.

11. Diane Ravitch, *Reign of Error* (New York: Knopf Doubleday, 2013).

12. Leon Botstein, *Jefferson's Children: Education and the Promise of American Culture* (New York: Doubleday, 1997), 223.

7

PRINCIPLES, VALUES, AND STEWARDSHIP

Democracy, taken in its narrower, purely political sense, suffers from the fact that those in economic and political power possess the means for molding public opinion to serve their own class interests. The democratic form of government in itself does not automatically solve problems; it offers, however, a useful framework for their solution. Everything depends ultimately on the political and moral qualities of the citizenry.

—Albert Einstein

Devoid of philosophical principles and values, society diminishes and decays. Values are the foundation for goodness, integrity, and virtue. Change comes through the power of ideals emerging from the commitment of individuals and a civil dialogue about them.

According to historian James MacGregor Burns, American purpose was informed by two values. "One is the pursuit of liberty as apotheosized in the Declaration of Independence, protected in the Bill of Rights, appealed to by the abolitionists, encoded and guaranteed, after many diversions and vagaries, by the Supreme Court. The other is equality, also proclaimed in the Declaration, reaffirmed by the struggle for emancipation, protected, as to race, in the Fourteenth and Fifteenth Amendments, appealed to by workers, farmers, and other disadvantaged groups during the nineteenth and early twentieth centuries."[1]

America faced, and continues to do so, conflict over these values. Confrontations about the rights of individuals and those of government, as well as the right of equal opportunity, persist. As times change and the nation evolves technologically, economically, and socially, disputes over rights and values will continue. They are the basis for maintaining political and social integrity, even though transformational change alters socioeconomic and other conditions.

At times, rights themselves conflict.[2] Sometimes the rights in the Constitution and the Bill of Rights create clashes. For example, with the publication of the Pentagon Papers in 1971 the government sued the *New York Times*, claiming that the reports endangered national security. The *New York Times* countered that the public had a right to know and that freedom of the press should be upheld. The court basically had to review the conflict between national security versus freedom of the press: they came down on the side of free press. People must exert themselves to ensure that government and society act with integrity to values and American ideals.

Former senator Gary Hart indicated ideas are the foundation of American government and culture that empower citizens. In essence, the principles and values provide a "perpetual revolution of generations" because "values produce beliefs; beliefs are the source of principles; principles are the basis for ideology; ideology produces policies; policies are the foundation for programs. There is, in other words, a logic to the development of ideas that govern our lives."[3]

Empowerment brings choices and requires productive involvement. To be involved, individuals must understand where they stand personally and define and interpret their principles and values. Citizens must also learn and comprehend the nation's principles so they can be implemented properly and credibly in an indefinite future.

Peter Drucker[4] discussed the importance of individuals determining their core values, because they are significant in their behavior and self-management. They ultimately affect how and what individuals determine their life's course to be. In addition, they direct where they belong in terms of education, interests, and priorities. Value conflicts arise because some personal values may clash with the values of employers, friends, family, or organizations. How these conflicts are addressed—civilly or uncivilly—is derived from personal values.

Everyone at one time or another confronts their individual integrity. Determining "who you are" is fundamental to lead a life of honor and genuineness. A big influence on developing personal and social responsibility emanates from early family life. Learning civility or incivility starts at an early age.

Peterson and Seligman have stated that civic identities, responsibilities, and values of young people are greatly influenced by family: "The early years of childhood are formative, and family values play a key role in the socialization of social responsibility. . . . To the extent that families emphasized attending to others and their needs, not just to the self, youth incorporated in their own identities the values of social responsibility and citizenship standards to live by."[5]

PRINCIPLES AND VALUES

The terms *principles* and *values* are frequently used interchangeably. The word *principle* comes from the Latin term *principium*, which means "source, origin, beginning." Principle is "a primary truth that formed the basis for other beliefs and then to mean a rule for ethical conduct."[6]

Value is rooted in the Latin word for strength and material worth, which gradually came to mean intrinsic worth and then absorbed a psychological/sociological meaning concerning acceptable behavior. Hence, while principles are fixed and absolute, values, like beliefs, may change as societal or personal needs and circumstances evolve.

Principles drive values and goals and act as anchors during difficult and conflicting times. The major political parties may have different values, but both espouse the same principles. While there may be agreement in principle, conflicts and collisions occur over the values and approaches defined to achieve the principle.

Covey states, "Principles are like lighthouses. They are natural laws that cannot be broken."[7] He believes that principles are the territory and values are the maps. Principles drive values and goals, but the course to achieve them may be different. Truth, freedom, equality, and justice are principles. How they are attained may differ based on values, which defines a person's perspective on matters of principle.

Principles must be applied equally to everyone regardless of political affiliation or viewpoint. Too often in the circle of politics and opinion, a principle is applied to one person but ignored in the behavior of another. Both Democrats and Republicans are guilty of this selected accountability to principle based on political opinions, identity politics, and power.

Ethics are the moral standards for determining and evaluating the rightness or wrongness of behavior, policy, and standards.[8] For example, individuals may share the same value of achieving economic or social success. For some, the expectation would be for them to work hard and acquire appropriate skills and compete. However, others may deceive and cheat their way to achieve their goal.

Ethics in leadership, as well as in interpersonal and civic interactions, determine credibility. In *Bad Leadership*, Barbara Kellerman[9] defines the qualities leaders and others in authority have. Ethical leaders place the followers' needs first, and they exemplify and live virtues like courage to promote the common good. They are not self-centered and interested strictly in their own personal interest.

Public officials are answerable to citizens. However, citizens are accountable, in part, for the ethics of their leaders because they elect them and as a matter of principle hold them accountable. Citizens must demonstrate the courage to do so and engage and confront leaders on behalf of what is right ethically and in the interest of the common good. Looking the other way or deferring because of party affiliation or dogma lack honesty and integrity. Citizens who do so are a part of the problem. They must speak out and mobilize others to stop corruption and dishonor.

Employees sometimes face difficult ethical dilemmas (for example, when employees are expected to behave in ways that are contrary to their personal or professional values). In these cases, they may have to courageously apply their conscience and refuse to conduct themselves in ways they feel are not ethical. Obviously, there are repercussions for this stance, but followers or citizens are obligated not only to themselves but also to the larger community. Civil disobedience is an example, as stated in Martin Luther King's letter in 1963 from the Birmingham jail.

Negotiating on principles is not feasible in these situations. Joseph Badaracco states, "People should do the right thing, not half of it. They should tell the whole truth, not half-truths. They should be fair all the time, not just on Mondays, Wednesdays, or Fridays."[10] Two positive principles colliding create very difficult situations. How can people meet somewhere between principles like freedom or equality?

DEFINING MOMENTS: RIGHT VERSUS RIGHT

Many people think discord is always about a right versus wrong conflict. Seldom do individuals see conflict as a clash between two positive principles. Deciding between two "right" principles is challenging and uncomfortable because they "reveal, they test, and they shape."[11]

On the national level, an example of a "right versus right" decision is the collision of two constructive rights—the right to privacy versus the right to security. This conflict raises issues of the prospect of less privacy of telephone, internet, and other communications to ensure national security. To some, privacy rights are a priority, and they would argue that other ways to ensure security must be found. To others, security comes first. Safety trumps privacy as far as they are concerned, and sacrificing some privacy is acceptable. Finding the balance is not always easy: to some, the balance cannot be found. Falling on either side of a conflict of principle produces discord and debate and sometimes results in fragmentation and discord.

Conflicts of right versus right decisions reveal the basic values of individuals facing the situation. The assumption is individuals understand the principles they hold in order to see the possible confrontation between two of them. Comprehending the situation accurately and determining the strength of their commitment to the two particular values in conflict are important.

In these situations, being cognizant of and sensitive to the interpretation of others is necessary. The level of commitment to their values also is at play. Even if the values of others are synchronous, which principle takes precedence for each individual may vary. Some may fall on separate sides (for example, privacy over security or vice versa).

Finally, making the decision stressing one "right" principle over another "right" principle has to be played forward. Analyzing the details of the long-term effects of this conflict is critically important in making a choice of one over another. Defining moments are born from these choices.

Defining moments frequently come down to making decisions over the conflict of two "rights," which are difficult and tear at the heart and intellect. They test commitment and priorities. And they quickly become symbolic decisions personally and to others because they clarify the individual's life and priorities.

These moments clarify character by revealing whether they live up to principles or simply give them lip service: whether the individuals act on what is right to them and not on the desires of a group, peers, or associates. In these discussions, candor is necessary, along with realistic perspectives and even a dose of skepticism.

In addition, people in these situations should take time—slow down, step back, and reflect and think. Right versus right decisions pull people in several directions simultaneously. Ensuring that major issues do not become minor, or that minor issues become major, is important; otherwise, attention can be deflected from confronting the hard decisions because they are not given priority.

Understanding the principle and values at hand is fundamental. Knowing their origin and evolution is essential because without knowledge, interpretation and analysis can be faulty or purely speculative. With defining moments, knowledge and understanding matter.

For example, thinking clearly about justice is a given when acting as a citizen: going beyond platitudinous phrases and truly understanding what freedom of speech, the right to privacy, equal opportunity, and the pursuit of happiness really mean and involve are essential knowledge. Interpretation and implementation of national principles continues and must be discussed and debated, relying on sound and accurate knowledge and understanding.

As a citizen, considering the rights and beliefs of others is necessary in a civil society. Acting ethically and respecting the dignity of all people are important. Understanding that others also have the same autonomy to make choices highlights that agreement is not necessary, but understanding is. While there may be agreement that the two clashing principles of values are important, which one takes precedence may differ because of people's experience, comprehension, and perspective.

Citizenship demands a moral sense: discerning the difference between right and wrong, which is required to prepare children for the future in a dynamic society and defining moments. They will face issues that challenge their integrity and call for understanding and commitment to ethical standards.

STEWARDSHIP

Citizens in America are stewards of their country and its integrity. Civility is an aspect of stewardship and empowerment and should be modeled in all interactions and dilemmas.

Ethics are a part of stewardship, which "requires courage to face special interests, the economically connected, the politically powerful, and the criticism of pundits and the press. . . . Doing what is expedient takes less courage than doing what is right. Decisions and pressure are part of public life, but those decisions should look to the future and to the common good."[12]

Stewardship requires an understanding that only in a civil context can people see others and understand their perspective so society and governance can be improved.

"Reverence is a form of stewardship. To be a good steward is to leave your home, relationships, community, organization, and world in better shape than you found them. To make that vital effort requires emotion and feeling. Passion and its sometimes difficult cousin, intensity, can mobilize and inspire others."[13]

Citizens must bring about the best and improve their communities and even work to heal any wounds or divisions that fragment them. Stewards use their talent and abilities to make positive contributions and move the community to a higher state of cohesion and wholeness. They have a sense of helping positive things to emerge by building capacity and eliminating the things that deplete energy and strength.

Citizenship in the United States moves far beyond dependency on higher powers or a select few. Dependency rests on the idea that individuals holding positions of authority know what is best for others. In actuality, those officeholders are dependent upon the will of the people.

Accountability requires a sense of ownership and responsibility for present conditions and the outcomes in the future. In reality, the answer to questions and concerns lies within each citizen and their willingness to stand up, respond, and be accountable for the well-being of the nation. Citizens must determine what it is they have to offer and what they wish to leave behind as a result of their efforts.

As stewards, citizens are accountable for the state of the nation and communities: whether there is a sense of unity or fractures or civility or incivility. The power of the ballot, speech, petition, and law, along with personal interaction and communication, are important in remedying coarse, unfair, and fragmented conditions.

THE DARK SIDE AND INCIVILITY

A dark side can surface in situations and politics. Dark Side leaders use authority and power for negative purposes. While stewardship holds to positive action and trusting relationships, there is a Dark Side characterized by fear, cynicism, and mistrust, which is fueled by anger and aggression. The Dark Side spawns resentment and incivility.

Dark Side leaders use the power of incivility to intimidate and oppress those who disagree with them. Deception and stigmatizing are used to coerce others. The power of personality is utilized to depersonalize and stereotype opponents. Fear frequently drives out logic and decorum.

Dark Side leaders apply attribution to deride and ascribe false and reprehensible motives to others through character assassination and doomsday projections and scenarios. Incivility, as a tool, deflects attention from the issues at hand to the focus of the incivility and its backlash.

The question is: What can citizens and leaders do in the face of Dark Side leadership and movements? As empowered citizens, it is their responsibility, at times, to lead by outrage. Outrage does not mean (and is not synonymous with) incivility. When power is abused and positive purposes ignored, citizens must stand up and use their moral authority—ideals, values, and ethics—to combat the destructive power and self-serving efforts of Dark Side leaders, who may be fellow citizens, politicians, or others. History demonstrates that when citizens fail to do so, tragic endings are the result.

Moral authority relies on persuasion. Getting others to challenge the efforts of those in leadership and other positions who lack integrity and prostitute values and standards is necessary. When the equal treatment and integrity of people are compromised, it is the obligation of citizens to stand up. The welfare of the community depends on an understanding of the interdependence of all citizens and people.

Civility means to engage and care in a respectful but forthright manner, raising issues of principle. Citizens have the power and moral authority to be stewards and care for their local communities. Thomas Sergiovanni stated, "Empowerment derives its full strength from being linked to purposing: everyone is free to do what makes sense, as long as people's decisions embody the values shared"[14] by the community. Outrage is not in any way the application of violence, but it does mean standing up, civilly expressing concerns, and making the case for why things are not in harmony with principles.

STANDING UP AND ENGAGING

As citizens, there is an obligation not to simply accept values but to question and challenge their application and their integrity in action and legislation. Understanding is not indoctrination because to understand requires discussion and debate.

For a country based on values, such as the right to life, privacy, free speech, and others, learning the philosophical principles inherent in them and how they apply to individuals in society requires thought, dialogue, and debate.

Debate requires critical thinking and, at times, there may not be a single-doctrinaire correct response. Working out the dilemmas of rights does not come down to blind acceptance of one interpretation. That is why there is a separation of powers and a Supreme Court detached from day-to-day politics.

When citizens have the freedom to think clearly about issues and challenge the practical application or solutions to them, they raise the question of whether the decisions have integrity with the nation's ideals. Difficult ethical questions may have more than one course or solution. American society depends on a citizenry that understands and has the individual recourse to debate principles and values collectively and the best way to uphold them.

Supreme Court Justice Holmes said the Constitution embodies "the principle of free thought—not free thought for those who agree with us but freedom for the thought that we hate."[15] Parker Palmer believes that the "American founders—despite the bigotry that limited their conception of who 'We the People' were—had the genius to establish the first form of government in which differences, conflict and tension were understood not as enemies of a good social order but as engines of a better social order."[16]

Children must understand and learn to become engaged with democratic values. Practicing democracy in school involves discussing issues and moving beyond hollow name-calling or labeling. They need to learn how to have a conversation about the United States and its values and examine the progress the country made to deliver them with integrity.

In addition, learning to serve others via school government or volunteer efforts gives students actual experience and knowledge of service and stewardship. The example of teachers who model values and stewardship are powerful role models.

Part of understanding America is comprehending how the "bonds of cohesion make us a nation rather than an irascible collection of unaffiliated groups." Arthur Schlesinger states, "Yet what has held the American people together in the absence of a common ethnic origin has been precisely a common adherence to ideals of democracy and human rights that, too often transgressed in practice, forever goad us to narrow the gap between practice and principle."[17]

The United States is unique in its formation, government, and expressed principles. A nation of immigrants coming from across the globe throughout history stay united only because these diverse people desire to live under its principles and values. *E pluribus unum* is not just a marketing slogan: it is the philosophical glue that binds the country together.

WHAT CITIZENS MUST KNOW

- Principles and values revitalize nation and people. They garner commitment to empowerment and positive citizenship in their pursuit and maintenance.
- America and citizens face conflict over values, their interpretation, and the clash between two positive principles.
- Values produce beliefs, beliefs are the source for principles, principles are the basis for ideology, ideology produces policies, and policies are the foundation for programs.
- Families have significant influence on the formation of social responsibility in children and the standards under which they live.
- Ethics are the foundation for formal and informal leadership and are the moral standards for determining and evaluating the rightness or wrongness of behavior, policy, and standards.

- Citizens, at times, must stand up and lead by outrage when unethical conduct, corruption, and dishonor are evident in social and political life.
- Defining moments are frequently the result of conflicts between two right principles.
- Citizens must learn the values under which the government and society operates and be able to assess when positive values clash and find the appropriate course and the implications of that decision.
- Stewardship requires courage and is the foundation for decisions people make in their role as citizens. Stewards work to make circumstances better than when they found them.
- A Dark Side exists when leaders and others use fear, cynicism, and aggression coupled with power for negative purposes to intimidate and oppress those who disagree with them.
- Children need to learn the principles and values that are the foundation of the nation and understand that the principle of free thought applies to all citizens regardless of whether the individual agrees with them.

NOTES

1. James MacGregor Burns, *Leadership* (New York: Harper Torch Books, 1979), 383–90.
2. "Civil Liberties and Civil Rights," American Government online, http://www.ushistory.org/gov/1-.asp.
3. Gary Hart, *The Good Fight* (New York: Random House, 1993), 41.
4. Peter Drucker, "Managing Oneself," in *On Managing Yourself* (Boston: Harvard Review Press, 2010), 16.
5. Christopher Peterson and Martin E. P. Seligman, *Character, Strengths, and Virtues* (American Psychological Association: Oxford University Press, 2004), 381–82.
6. William Safire, "On Language: Principle vs. Value," *New York Times*, August 12, 1984.
7. Stephen R. Covey, *The 7 Habits of Highly Effective People: Powerful Lessons in Personal Change* (RosettaBooks, 2013), 41.
8. Minessence Group, "Once the Difference between Values, Ethics, in Principles?" https://values-knowledge-base.blogspot.com/2011/12/whats-difference-between-values-ethics.html.

9. Barbara Kellerman, *Bad Leadership* (Boston: Harvard Business School Press, 2004), 34–36.

10. Joseph Badaracco, *Leading Quietly* (Boston: Harvard Business School Press, 2002), 148.

11. Joseph Badaracco, *Defining Moments* (Boston: Harvard Business School Press, 1997), 7.

12. George A. Goens, *The Fog of Reform* (Lanham, MD: Rowman & Littlefield, 2016), 50.

13. George A. Goens, *Soft Leadership for Hard Times* (Lanham, MD: Rowman & Littlefield, 2005), 21.

14. Thomas J. Sergiovanni, *Moral Leadership* (San Francisco, CA: Jossey-Bass, 1992), 129.

15. Arthur M. Schlesinger, *The Disuniting of America: Reflections on a Multicultural Society*, revised and enlarged edition (New York: W. W. Norton, 1998), 119.

16. Parker J. Palmer, *Healing the Heart of Democracy: Courage to Create Politics Worthy of the Human Spirit* (Hoboken, NJ: Wiley, 2014), xx.

17. Schlesinger, *The Disuniting of America*, 122.

8

REASON AND TRUTH

To be persuasive we must be believable; to be believable we must be credible; to be credible we must be truthful.

—Edward R. Murrow

Lieut. Kaffee: I want the truth!
Col. Jessup: You can't handle the truth!

—from the movie *A Few Good Men*

Edward R. Murrow's quote speaks clearly and simply about discourse and communication. In the movie *A Few Good Men*, Lieutenant Kaffee and Colonel Jessup's iconic repartee frames a courtroom debate around the search for truth. The legal system is based on "the truth, the whole truth, and nothing but the truth."

Truth is serious and affects all facets of life—personal, professional, and political. But what is truth? Perspective can color people's analysis and versions of things. Even if individuals describe events honestly as they see them, there are issues. Individuals observe the same incidents but describe and interpret them differently from their own perspective, history, and circumstances. From their viewpoint, they are honest in their descriptions of the events, but the accurate and definitive truth may not be as clear.

Individuals do not simply look at things through a strict cognitive and analytical lens. Feelings and attitudes, as well as philosophy, life experiences, and other circumstances, affect how things are heard, seen, and perceived. As a result, people portray the same event differently, not out of malice but because of their sensibility and mind-set. The attitude and behavior of the participants can also be a factor. Principled and truthful discussion is fundamental to a healthy democracy because without it, dependability and honesty are shattered and become extremely difficult to resurrect.

The basic issue in any communication is trust. Without a sense that the person is sincere and credible, trust will not exist. If the ability of the person to make reasoned judgments is lost, credibility is absent. Trust does not come with college degrees, titles, or past accomplishments. It is an intangible perception that can easily be destroyed by uncovering deceptions and agendas that do not comport to clear and impartial analysis. Nowadays, "spin" and the focus on personal advantage is prevalent in many aspects of life.

Determining fact from fiction, propaganda from reality, dishonesty from authenticity, and facts from falsehoods are necessary qualities in personal and social contexts. Citizens must have the ability to examine and scrutinize issues, proposals, campaign platforms, scientific conclusions, metrical data, and many other questions and circumstances.

Leadership, elections, and court decisions require credibility. Without it, the cloud of fabrication and deceit damages their integrity. Any shading of the truth damages veracity, and institutions can be shaken to the core if ethical and honorable behavior is breached.

Education is not only a quest for knowledge but also the search for truth. When power rests with citizens, they must have the knowledge and skills to assess statements and propositions and to sort through propaganda, deception, and outright lies.

Reason and logic matter for both individuals and the greater society. In the *Age of American Unreason*, Susan Jacoby states, "Two thirds of Americans cannot name the three branches of government or come up with the name of a single Supreme Court Justice . . . Americans who get the news primarily from television rather than newspapers know much less about the judicial system than newspaper readers. Two thirds of newspaper readers, but only 40% of television news watchers, know that the primary mission of the Supreme Court is to interpret the Constitution."[1]

Jacoby states that both dumbness and smartness have been defined "downward." As a result, it is easier to persuade people of the validity of extreme positions. Knowledge and the ability to think critically and to discriminate between factual errors and differences of opinion are requisites for understanding and accountability.

Today's society has tools and access to information unimaginable in times past. The printing press created a revolution in the ability to acquire and read books and other documents, opening the doors to ideas, philosophies, and treatises on a variety of subjects. Society benefited from access to and the discussion of values and philosophical principles, as well as exposure to the sciences, literature, history, politics, and news.

Literacy opens the doors to debate and, in practicality, change and reform. Ideas are powerful because they capture people's imaginations and intellects. Emotions and souls stir with hope and optimism. Reading critically and discerning viewpoints and strategies of argument become consequential. Many parents at one time or another have cautioned their children, "Just because it is written (or stated) doesn't make it so." Determining plausibility requires an open but discerning mind.

To some, a paradox exists. "Never have so many people had so much access to so much knowledge and yet have been so resistant to learning anything."[2] Nichols asserts that people lack basic information and the rules of evidence in making a logical argument. Discerning fact from fiction, propaganda from objectivity, and bias from impartiality become impossible without the ability to think critically.

Society is flooded with easy access to data, commentary, advice, opinions, news, documents, statistics, and particulars on a wide variety of content. In addition, a glut of propaganda and promotions presents "spin," disinformation, falsehoods, oversimplification, hype, and indoctrination.

In computer science and mathematics, the term *GIGO* was coined years ago—"garbage in, garbage out"—which means the quality of the output is determined by the quality of the input. The same is true in social and political discourse.

JUNK THOUGHT

One result is the expansion of "junk thought." "The defining characteristics of junk thought, which manifests itself in the humanities and social sciences as well as the physical sciences, are anti-rationalism and contempt for countervailing facts and expert opinion. It cannot be stressed enough that junk thought emanates from both the left and the right, even though each group—in academia, politics, and cultural institutions—accuses the other of being the sole source of irrationality."[3]

Frequently, according to Jacoby, junk thought uses the language of science and rationality to promote irrational conclusions. Just like junk food, it is easily accessible: simply click the mouse, open a site, and antirationalism is at hand. For example, one prime illustration is a story that chocolate helps people lose weight, which was based on falsehoods but received wide public attention because the sources of the story were not vetted. A quote attributed to P. T. Barnum may apply: "There's a sucker born every minute."

Junk thought does not discern between coincidence and causation but uses scientific language without concrete empirical evidence or logic. Innumeracy is a problem because individuals lack an understanding of statistical and mathematical concepts. Many people think that something is true if it spouts statistics. Because of lack of statistical knowledge, people presume that the inclusion of numerical data indicates that it must be true—after all, in their eyes "numbers don't lie." They appear so much more scientific and truthful than words alone.

In other cases, individuals choose selected data and facts—cherry pick—that support their position and leave out others that oppose it. While on the surface the facts are correct, the piece lacks integrity because all of the data are not presented or presented properly. Selected data frequently occurs in politics and debates. Cherry picking data and misinterpreting its impact and conclusions can prostitute good research.

Einstein famously stated, "Not everything that can be counted counts, and not everything that counts can be counted." Mark Twain likewise said, "There are lies, damned lies, and statistics." These two quotes highlight the problem.

THE MEDIA

The media thrives on conflict and controversy. Infotainment and the celebrity culture dominate as viewership, and ratings are the goal. Exploring issues in depth is not the priority, and details and accuracy are sacrificed for ratings. Many problems and issues are nuanced and complex, requiring more than superficial knowledge, sound bites, or euphemisms to comprehend. The line between journalism and entertainment blurs particularly if news is skewed to what the audience wants, rather than what citizens need to know.

Americans today supposedly live in the "information age" and are involved in the "information explosion." In the past, television and radio represented the media. No longer. Computers, cell phones, iPads, and video monitors are prevalent everywhere, and sometimes annoyingly so. The assumption is that access to media is what matters. More of everything, however, does not mean higher quality or clearer thought. These are great concerns.

The classic book by Neil Postman cited the hazards of contemporary media and the development of an educated citizenry. In *Amusing Ourselves to Death*, he stated, "When the population gets distracted by trivia, when cultural life is redefined as a perpetual round of entertainments, when serious public conversation becomes a form of baby-talk, when, in short, a people become an audience and their public business a vaudeville act, then the nation finds itself at risk; culture-death is a clear possibility."[4] In all of this, of course, euphemisms prevail; a prime illustration includes the late comedian George Carlin's classic examples that "lies" become "misinformation," "deaths of civilians" become "collateral damage," and "being fired" becomes a "career transition."

Postman warns that in this media age there is no longer discussion or widespread public understanding. He asks poignant basic questions about information:

> What is information? Or more precisely, what are information? What are its various forms? What conceptions of intelligence, wisdom, and learning does each form insist upon? What conceptions does each form neglect or mock? What are the main psychic effects of each form? What is the relation between information and reason? What is the kind of information that best facilitates thinking? Is there a moral bias to each information form? What does it mean to say that there is too much information? How would one know? What redefinitions of important cultural meanings do new sources, speeds, context, and forms of information require? Does television, for example, give new meaning to "piety," to "patriotism," to "privacy"? Does television give new meaning to "judgment" or to "understanding"? How do different forms of information persuade? Is a newspaper's "public" different from television's "public"? How do different information forms dictate the type of content that is expressed?[5]

Cynicism exists regarding the media, its truthfulness, and objectivity. A "free press" and journalism has always been a pillar of American democracy. Relying on the judgment of journalists has been pivotal in presenting the "first history" of issues and events.

The Society of Professional Journalists "believe[s] that public enlightenment is the forerunner of justice and the foundation of democracy. Ethical journalism strives to ensure the free exchange of information that is accurate, fair and thorough. An ethical journalist acts with integrity."[6] The ethical code has four major areas:

- Seek the truth and report it
- Minimize harm
- Act independently
- Be accountable and transparent

Getting the facts right is a cardinal principle of journalism. Accuracy, fairness, and impartiality are traditional journalistic standards. Minimizing harm is the realization that what journalists publish or broadcast may be hurtful to individuals and institutions and that their words and impressions can have a large impact on people. Accuracy, then, is absolutely critical. Gossip, speculation, and hearsay have no place. Unsubstantiated reports and their notoriety get great emphasis. Unfortunately, journalistic errors do not get the same scrutiny.

A major concept of every profession is accountability: journalists must hold themselves accountable when they commit errors, and they must be independent and not act in the interests of corporate, political, or other special interests. Ensuring that sources are reliable and honest is critical to credibility and reliability. Journalists must be dogged in certifying information as factual and independent. The interpretation of information is also essential in journalism because, at times, the explanation and meaning of stories can be wrong and conflicting.

The past ethos of print journalism was not to entice the audience's desires for amusement and entertainment or manipulation for ratings. Rather, the press—the Fourth Estate—was to report and be a check and balance on the government and its activities and operations, not a medium for political or corporate exploitation and profit.

The media, as presented today, is free of the professional responsibilities to which journalists have been committed. The pressure to be first, to focus on "if it bleeds, it leads," and to report what people want, rather than need, endangers those principles. Now anyone or any group can post things to raise issues, gather support, and garner commitment based, not necessarily on facts and reason, but on propaganda and indoctrination.

The media panders to short attention spans and focuses on suffering and novelty, not on dialogue and reflection. Speed and laser-focused attention to stories of violence, competition, or conflict dominate. Thoughtful deliberation takes depth and time that ratings do not allow. Even shows committed to analysis devote very little time to discussing complex issues, and, in many cases, the commentators just pitch partisan views.

TECHNOLOGICAL IMPACT

The internet presents other issues. Some 62 percent of Americans get their news through social media. Most of it is via Facebook, and a large percentage of it is through online traffic flows through Google.[7] This information spreads quickly, and the boundaries of fact or fiction corrode and "fake news" gains traction by using fabrication or manipulated content. In addition, these sites are available instantaneously, and time for contemplation becomes consumed by texting "likes" and other social media tags. Journalism was to be an institution not of irrational rants and uncivil reaction but of civil analysis and discussion. Reasoned research was the hallmark of getting the story and getting it right based on journalistic standards and values.

Mark Epstein, in an article in the *Wall Street Journal*, stated that Google and Facebook "control how millions of people find their news. Americans are far likelier, collectively, to encounter articles via search engines and social media than on a news site's home page . . . A Pew survey this summer found that most popular social-media sites for getting news are Facebook, YouTube (owned by Google), Twitter (which has a Google partnership), and Instagram (owned by Facebook). No more than 5% of Americans use another social-media platform to get news."[8] He states that the "tech duopoly" dominance threatens the "marketplace of ideas." Controlling the overproviding of information can be dangerous: whoever controls it can direct thought and perspective.

Other potential hazards exist as Facebook and other sites sort information through algorithms that determine suggested content and influence based on what individuals see, explore, buy, or read. Amazon and Netflix use them to make recommendations on books and films. Algorithms nudge individuals—both adults and children—in their choices and selections based on past expressions and behavior.

In a paradoxical way, Foer indicated, "humans are comfortable with ignorance, but they hate feeling deprived of information."[9] In that vein, major newspapers have adopted what Foer calls "snackable content"— charts, videos, quick items with limited or frivolous content—that appeals to those who are bored or killing time. In addition, narcissistic attitudes and cynical knee-jerk reactions block any interest in exploring issues and understanding the philosophy, principles, concepts, and history behind them.

Propaganda and skewed stories are obstacles to citizens' need for the truth. Generally technology has been perceived as a force for good, one that should make the world a better place. It was originally seen as a neutral force, making information and data available and communication easier. However, technology and its application is not value neutral. Individuals can post and make themselves heard without reliance on others. Standards and civility are not always applied, and rumors and falsehoods are posted without forethought but with great emotion. Technology can also have serious pitfalls and dark sides.

In actuality, Big Tech has created problems for citizens and the operation of democracy. The internet evolved from a "decentralized network into one dominated by a few giant technology companies: Facebook, Amazon, Netflix, and Alphabet's Google—the so-called FANGs. This new hierarchy is motivated primarily by the desire to sell—above all, to sell the data that their users provide."[10] Online advertising is prolific.

The initiation to provide news that holds the attention of users has resulted in "fake news," and people obtain selected information based on their previous site selections. Algorithmic behavior can close rather than open new perspectives. In a sense, algorithms can reduce the scope of sources and ideas and contribute to creating a silo effect.

Many worship at the altar of technology and favor its impact on education and learning. The assumption is that technology will make people smarter. However, Adrian Ward of the University of Texas at Austin found that cell phones produced distractions, making concentration more difficult, as well as impeding reasoning and performance. "Dr. Ward suspected that our attachment to our phones has grown so intense that their mere presence might diminish our intelligence."[11]

As technological gadgets make accessing data easier, people's knowledge may dwindle because of the "Google effect," in which people "offload memories to the 'cloud,' undermining the impulse to ensure that some important facts get inscribed into 'our biological memory banks.'"[12]

Reliance on cell phones and other technology can cause a "brain drain" that can "diminish such vital skills as learning, logical reasoning, abstract thought, problem solving, and creativity."[13] All of these cognitive skills are fundamental to critical thinking and assessing data and information.

Citizens must be able to perform these cognitive functions and not rely simply on technology or the analysis of others. *1984* was a popular science fiction book, but today the addictive effect of technology and its parsing of information may not be as much fiction as people think. "Alternative facts," "disinformation," and "fake news" are examples of the distortion of truth. They assert that truth is pliable and can be interpreted to conform to a particular belief, opinion, point of view, or philosophy.

Thinking is and always will remain the critical skill necessary to avoid totalitarian and autocratic influence or demagoguery. Keeping a democratic republic well informed also requires a citizenry that is educated in thinking skills and moral and ethical standards. Understanding subtleties of language and nuances of argument are indispensable to discern content and intent, information from opinion, and truth from fiction. Civil society requires a means to discern truth from fabrication and opinion.

KNOWLEDGE, OPINION, AND BELIEFS

Knowledge is the power that empowers citizens. Knowledge and opinions are not identical and equal. Knowledge must meet distinct criteria, while opinions do not. In reality knowledge cannot be false. Opinions, by contrast, can be true or false. If opinions do meet these criteria for truth, they are no longer opinions.

All opinions are not equal, and feelings are not facts. They exist, but they may not be accurate or based on knowledge or reason, nor are they always in harmony or congruent.

Interpreting the intent of facts or opinions forms feelings. Some interpretations may be totally off base from what the communicator intended. Even if the facts are correct, how they are stated can create misinterpretations and discord. The result of this can be confusion, vigorously articulated politically and socially through anger and incivility.

While each vote is of equal value and importance in America, each opinion is not. As issues become complex, expert advice and dialogue become important. Learning, contemplating, and listening in these times are essential for correct analysis and decision making. Reliable sources are necessary, particularly in finding objective and hard truth.

Knowledge is indispensable because people must understand the principles of liberty, equality, individual rights, consent of the governed, the rule of law, and others. Junk thought and "false knowledge" are serious threats to civility and democracy. False knowledge is an oxymoron: a total contradiction in terms in an Orwellian way. But if it is accepted, it can be damaging to principles and people.

Philosopher Mortimer Adler defines the criteria for knowledge: "When the criteria for calling anything knowledge are such exacting criteria as the certitude, incorrigibility, and immutability of the truth that is known, then the few things that are knowledge stand far apart from everything that might be called opinion. . . . A self-evident truth is one that states something the opposite of which is impossible to think."[14] An example of a self-evident truth is that a finite whole is greater than any of its component parts.

Adler specifies that certitude, incorrigibility, and immutability are the criteria for knowledge that differentiates it from opinions. Some opinions, however, are stronger than others. There may be "sufficient probative force" to justify claiming an opinion *may* be true *at the time*. Later evidence may prove that perspective to be false.[15]

Individuals have personal perspectives and prejudices that influence their positions and attitudes, placing them in the category of opinion because they do not have any foundation in evidence or reason. Yet individuals spout them full force even though they totally lack incorrigibility, immutability, and certitude.

When individuals say "I believe . . ." they are really signifying that there is some level of doubt in their position. For example, people know that two plus two equals four with certitude; they do not simply have a belief that it is true. People, however, can believe that there are unidentified flying objects piloted by aliens. Until there is factual evidence, this will remain a belief.

Another kind of knowledge concerns moral philosophy, according to Adler. Moral values such as right and wrong or good or evil are about what individuals ought or ought not do. Individuals who think that something is the right thing to do amounts to indicating that it ought to be done.

Not everyone agrees with the veracity of moral values. Some indicate that they are absolute standards of right and wrong, while others find that moral judgments are simply a person's opinion, predilection, or bias.

Adler states, "Knowledge is not the highest of the intellectual goals. A higher value is understanding and, beyond that, wisdom."[16]

TRUTH AND LYING

"Fake knowledge," "false news," and "junk science" permeate discussions in today's media. All of these are examples of instability because of their deceit and disrespect to the standards of communication and democracy. As a result, people become exasperated and lose faith in the integrity of news agencies and other institutions.

At one time or another, most parents have had a discussion with their children about lying. "Are you telling the truth?" is a phrase most children hear at some point in their lives. Truth and honesty obviously have connections, but, as Mortimer Adler states, "When a person speaks truthfully it follows necessarily that what he thinks is true in fact."[17]

Then there is the question of ignorance. In other words, is it possible for a person to truthfully express a falsehood because in their mind it is factual and they believe it to be accurate? Individuals may think what they say is true. There is no deceit in thinking and saying something not founded on facts if the person believes it is true. It is just ignorance. Ideally, in these circumstances facts will override ignorance, and truth will surface and be accepted.

Lying, however, has an element of conscious deceit: "There is a lack of correspondence between what one thinks and what one says."[18] In this case, there is a discrepancy between what a person states and what the individual is actually thinking. Speaking truthfully, in other words, is when what we think and what we speak conform.

In contemporary communication, the intentional reporting of things that individuals or groups know are not factual is lying. Deliberately and knowingly relaying things that are distortions, skewed interpretations, or intentional fabrications are off limits for speaking or writing truthfully.

Pessimism about government and politics rests in large part on the outlook that this is how politicians and interest groups communicate. Communicating and parsing what people desire, not what they need to know, is a form of lying.

In face-to-face discourse, two people have the opportunity to ask questions and determine the interpretation and definition of terms. This is important and cannot be done easily in texting or certainly not on Twitter. Time and patience are necessary to determine the connection between what the individual says and its integrity to their thinking and perspective.

Frequently, individuals use conventional wisdom in the positions under the belief that it is true. The phrase *conventional wisdom*, made famous by economist John Kenneth Galbraith, is a body of generally accepted ideas, concepts, or judgments. Conventional wisdom, however, is not necessarily true. For example, in the early 1950s, it was conventional wisdom by most doctors that smoking was not a hazard to one's health.

Conventional wisdom exists in all fields. "The hallmark of conventional wisdom is acceptability. It has the approval of those to whom it is addressed. There are many reasons why people like to hear articulated that which they approve. It serves the ego: the individual has the satisfaction of knowing that other and more famous people share his conclusions. To hear what he believes is also a source of reassurance. The individual knows he is supported in his thoughts."[19]

Conventional wisdom, in other words, is meant to accommodate to the audience's view of the world—what the audience finds most acceptable. Accepting conventional wisdom as a truth reduces or minimizes friction and conflict but may fail the truth test and can lead to erroneous positions and actions.

The use of polls and surveys formulates and defines what the conventional wisdom is on a variety of topics. However, there can be more than one conventional wisdom phrase on the same topic. How poll and survey questions are asked can skew the results.

Misinformation and disinformation exist; sometimes a result of what individuals think is common sense. In the past, common sense assumed that the Sun revolved around the Earth. Today some claim that people use only 10 percent of their brains. Can that really be determined? Phrases and comments, as well as conventional wisdom, can be based on things other than concrete knowledge and facts.

THE SEARCH FOR TRUTH

What is true? How does one know what moves beyond strictly opinion and propaganda to the sphere of truth?

Professional journalists have an obligation to observe carefully and impartially, assess and utilize reliable and responsible sources, confirm or ignore rumors, and provide the opportunity for individuals cited in the story an opportunity to refute issues and statements.

The format for news stories generally answers the following questions: Who? What? Where? Why? How? How do we know? These questions are geared to assist in credible and impartial reporting.

The internet has no editorial filters or checks for accuracy or impartiality. Anyone can post opinions, speculation, or propaganda. Before the internet people relied on journalists and newspapers for information, which had a system to check the accuracy of stories. Some newspaper's reputations were built on strict editorial standards and review—even those that had a liberal or conservative slant. The *New York Times* slogan, "All the News That's Fit to Print," certainly intimated that some news was not "fit" to print.

According to Howard Gardner, young people prefer to get their "news" from reading blogs, particularly from sources with which they agree. In a sense, some individuals reside in valleys of opinion that simply echo their point of view. In addition, comedians have become a source of determining what is news: infotainment and satire geared to particular viewpoints do not provide deep insight beyond parody, innuendo, and opinion. Quips are not in-depth insights: many are just stereotypes based on popularity and increasing an audience with specific groups.

Gardner states, "How best can we establish the status of truth in a postmodern, digital era? By showing the power but also the limitations of sensory knowledge. By explaining the methods whereby the several disciplines—mathematics, science, history—go about arriving at their accounts of the world and arriving at their respective truths. By demonstrating how we evaluate disciplinary evidence—and the evidence from multiple disciplines—in determining truth value."[20]

Philosophically, the answer to what is truth would seem easy. Either something is true and exists in reality or it is false and does not exist. In a simple way, Adler states, "The definition of truth is the agreement of the mind with reality."[21]

Certainly reason is a part of using the mind to decipher the truth in the world. Michael Lynch indicates that "truth is objective: that it is good to believe what is true; that truth is a worthy goal of inquiry, and that truth is worth caring about for its own sake."[22] He expresses the idea that truth is a value, and if people don't care about the truth, they languish in ambiguity, fail to speak up, turn away from issues, do not ask questions, fudge data, and close their minds. "Not caring about the truth is a type of cowardice."

The search for truth demands action. Education is about pursuing the truth. All educated people should question, reflect, and study to find the objective truth and reality in the sciences and other academic areas. In some cases, discoveries may supplant what previously was thought and accepted to be true.

In matters of truth, dispute is fruitful. When examining the truth of opinions, proposals, and judgments, arguing with those who disagree can be enlightening. Too frequently today, people abandon the discussion, thereby deserting the pursuit of truth. A civil debate can uncover assumptions, facts, or philosophical dispositions that threaten or divert the search for truth.

Anxiety arises when there is a vacuum of truthful information, raising emotions, one of which is fear.

> Fear germinates from the anxiety of uncertainty or faulty or scarce communication. Then, creating illusions that go far beyond the realm of reality is easy and jeopardizes security. People become insecure and they create scenarios around their worst fears; they take their nastiest

imaginings and explode them into dire predictions. In most things in life, our worst fears never play out. Things are not as bad as we think, and silver linings and opportunities do appear in times of trial. With illusions, however, there are no silver linings: just gloom and doom. [23]

Illusions presented to the public via technology and media pump emotions, generate rage, and foster incivility. Perceptions are created that drive out logic and compassion, destroying any opportunity for reasoned discussion or dialogue.

Parker Palmer stated, "When we allow emotions to trump the intellect, we swallow 'facts' that are demonstrably untrue, letting them fly around unchallenged in a mockery of civic discourse, supporting public figures who promote fictions to further their own cause." [24]

Palmer also cautions against individuals allowing the media "exclusive rights to define our political world" because the result is "almost certain to end up with a distorted sense of reality and deformed habits of the heart." [25]

WHAT CITIZENS MUST KNOW

- Citizens must be able to check the veracity of comments, opinion, and knowledge.
- Critical, complex, and skeptical thinking skills are essential for citizens.
- Schools must focus on thinking skills, determining points of view, and establishing the authenticity and authority of sources, as well as the accurate use of metrics and data.
- Citizens must master basic information about American government and politics. They must check sources of information and use research skills to monitor and review the professionalism and credibility of sources.
- Citizens must find and use sources that provide depth of information on issues and programs affecting the country's welfare.
- Schools must provide students with the ability to evaluate sources of information and determine their strengths and limitations.
- Citizens must be concerned about the diversity of sources of their information and the concerns and problems of a few corporate sources controlling it.

- Citizens must have the ability to discern "fake news" and lying from actual knowledge and truth. Skepticism is not a negative when it comes to determining truthfulness of articles and opinion.
- Determining the perspectives and attitudes of sources is important to citizens along with being able to discern the interpretation of reporters, columnists, and sources of their positions and comments.
- A civil society requires means to determine the truth. Incivility threatens the prospect of doing so.
- Citizens must have clear criteria for defining truth and apply it in meeting their civic duty.
- Citizens must discern the difference between truth, opinion, lying, and ignorance.

NOTES

1. Susan Jacoby, *The Age of American Unreason* (New York: Vintage, 2009), 299.

2. Tom Nichols, *The Death of Expertise: The Campaign against Established Knowledge and Why It Matters* (Oxford: Oxford University Press, 2017), 2.

3. Jacoby, *The Age of American Unreason*, 211–15.

4. Neil Postman, *Amusing Ourselves to Death: Public Discourse in the Age of Show Business* (New York: Penguin, 2005).

5. Postman, *Amusing Ourselves to Death*, 2596.

6. Society of Professional Journalists, SPJ Code of Ethics, https://www.spj.org/ethicscode.asp.

7. Franklin Foer, *World without Mind: The Existential Threat of Big Tech* (New York: Penguin, 2017), 5.

8. Mark Epstein, "The Google-Facebook Duopoly Threatens Diversity of Thought," *Wall Street Journal*, December 18, 2017, https://www.wsj.com/articles/the-google-facebook-duopoly-threatens-diversity-of-thought-1513642519.

9. Epstein, "The Google-Facebook Duopoly," 138.

10. Niall Ferguson, "In Praise of Hierarchy," *Wall Street Journal*, January 6, 2018.

11. Nicholas Carr, "How Smartphones Hijack Our Minds," *Wall Street Journal*, October 6, 2017.

12. Daniel M. Wegner and Adrian F. Ward, "The Internet Has Become the External Hard Drive of Our Memories," *Scientific American*, December 1, 2013.

13. Carr, "How Smartphones Hijack Our Minds."

14. Mortimer Adler, *Ten Philosophical Mistakes* (New York: Touchstone Books, 1987), 85.

15. Adler, *Ten Philosophical Mistakes*, 86.

16. Adler, *Ten Philosophical Mistakes*, 107.

17. Mortimer J. Adler, *How to Think about Great Ideas: From the Great Looks of Western Civilization* (New York: Open Court, 2000), 3.

18. Adler, *How to Think about Great Ideas*, 3.

19. John Kenneth Galbraith, *The Affluent Society* (New York: Houghton Mifflin Harcourt, 1998), 9.

20. Howard Gardner, *Truth, Beauty, and Goodness Reframed: Education for the Virtues and the Age of Truthiness and Twitter* (New York: Basic Books, 2012), 35.

21. Mortimer J. Adler, *The Great Ideas* (New York: Macmillan, 1992), 868.

22. Michael P. Lynch, *True to Life: Why Truth Matters* (Cambridge, MA: MIT Press, 2004), 4–5.

23. George A. Goens, *Soft Leadership for Hard Times* (Lanham, MD: Rowman & Littlefield, 2005), 122.

24. Parker J. Palmer, *Healing the Part of Democracy: The Courage to Create Politics Worthy of the Human Spirit* (Hoboken, NJ: Wiley, 2014), 54.

25. Palmer, *Healing the Part of Democracy*, 153.

9

CITIZENSHIP AND CIVILITY

So we are where we are today. We are where we are because whenever we had a choice to make, we have chosen the alternative that required the least effort at the moment.

—Walter Lippman

When one succeeds in the search for identity, one has found the answer not only to the question "who am I" but to a lot of other questions too: What must I live up to? What are my obligations? To what must I commit myself?

—John W. Gardner

The right to vote is sometimes taken for granted or not exercised because of apathy, ignorance, or cynicism. "The two—universal suffrage and universal schooling—are inextricably bound together. The one without the other is a perilous delusion. Suffrage without schooling produces mobocracy, not democracy—not rule of law, not constitutional government by the people as well as for the people."[1] Knowledge and education are vital requisites for not only democracy but also civility.

Equal opportunity in education is significant simply because it translates into the prospect of equal participation as citizens. Children of all socioeconomic classes and backgrounds require and deserve the same education in content and access. Without it, they will not be able to participate knowledgeably and with equal standing as citizens.

Civic empowerment and engagement requires education. Equity in access to education is important because it allows children from all social classes and racial and ethnic backgrounds the freedom and equal opportunity to express themselves in government and civic issues. Without knowledge, equal opportunity is not possible in all facets of life, including citizenship. Being a pawn or a passive observer is not in harmony with the country's principles.

Citizens' lives should not be compromised because of inaccessibility to education.

> Individuals in our society who do not possess the levels of skill, literacy, and training essential to this new era will be effectively disenfranchised, not simply from the material rewards that accompany competent performance, but also from the chance to participate fully in our national life. A high level of shared education is essential to be a free, democratic society and to the fostering of a common culture, especially in a country that prides itself on pluralism and individual freedom. [2]

Citizenship requires a common educational background in the principles of the nation and the standards of democracy. In this regard, civic empowerment requires a common education to understand how government functions for students of all social strata: "There is compelling evidence that many students, especially low-income students of color, are getting little if any civic education. We have a profound civic empowerment gap . . . between low-income citizens of color, on the one hand, and middle-class and wealthy white citizens, on the other."[3]

Knowledge, information, and insight are essential to make informed choices. Acting responsibly requires understanding the United States and its history and values. Without this, citizens cannot assess the choices they have politically or socially.

Subtle and dramatic transformations are evident in most facets of people's lives. Each generation experienced shifts of this nature, and each had to step up and provide leadership. To do so, all citizens need the requisite knowledge and wisdom.

The pursuit of values and ideas and dedication to their realization results in consequential transformations. Integrity to principle, not just economic or personal self-interest, is extremely powerful in uniting people. When "addressing fundamental questions of human nature, values help to clarify the relations between individualism and collectivism, self-interest and altruism, liberty and equality—issues at the heart of political conflict—and in the process established a leadership agenda for action."[4]

Society is regenerated by civilly discussing the virtues on which society stands. Moral education is required: discussing goodness, truth, liberty, justice, equality, and beauty—the six great ideas—and the various perspectives around which they are evaluated and achieved.

The question is: What is civil? Amitai Etzioni states that "civility has been used in different ways, most commonly it is referred to the need to deliberate in a civil manner about the issues the society faces, and to sustain the intermediary bodies that stands between the individual and the state."[5] He asserts that acting in a civil manner is not entirely sufficient. A virtuous society also requires a core of shared values.

Civility does not mean walking on thin ice fearful of speaking or expressing ideas. However, it does require respecting others and their right of self-expression. Valuing differences is essential. There is never a time when everyone thinks alike, and certainly no two individuals are the same: they bring differences in philosophies, upbringing, attitudes, and values to the discussion.

DELIBERATIVE DISCUSSIONS

Deliberative discussions and conscious thought, as well as objective analysis, require reason. An open mind is required because vested interests may get in the way and interpretations and standards conflict. Freedom to think brings freedom to see things differently. Democracy ensures the right to disagree and, hopefully, through that disagreement find the possibility of common ground and creative solutions.

Deliberative discussions bring people together to investigate a shared issue with the possibility of examining consequences and finding solutions. Each individual brings possibilities and perspectives that can lead to the group coming to a reasoned solution. Deliberative discussions require that individuals[6]:

- Do not demonize one another
- Do not deliberately disrespect or insult the other group or their commitment
- Use the language of needs and interests rather than the language of rights
- Ask questions

- Leave some issues out of the debate in order to narrow the discussion and build on foundations

Participation across the political spectrum and respectful discourse are indispensable. Incivility is crippling. Respectful discourse is essential. Hearing other people's stories makes them human, not an "ist" of some kind: perceiving individuals just as racists, feminists, sexists, facists, socialists, nationalists, populists, elitists, militarists, or other "ists." Labeling divides. Stereotypes frequently have a base in prejudice or ignorance that results in faulty or incomplete characterizations and justifications for support or condemnation.

People are unique individuals with a history, not just a member of a group. Lumping them into a stereotypical group is the same mentality that undergirds racism. It's the same mental set. Name-calling with global epithets and categorizing individuals by group strips them of humanity by condemning them by group identity and association.

Listening leads to understanding as to why people hold particular positions, even if agreement is not there. Raising fears is counterproductive and impedes any originality that might arise through conscious deliberation and discussion.

Nations, just as individuals, can damage connections and relationships through false information, self-interest, greed, and power mongering. Trust, then, is destroyed, along with any ties or connections and any perception of honesty.

"For the restoration of civic virtue—citizen participation in government—the citizen must first believe our government to be honest. Honesty here is meant to include not simply its public statements but also the basic integrity of its processes and individuals who legislate and administer."[7]

When government departments or officials betray the values of a democracy, they destroy the solidarity of the institution. If their conduct is incongruent with established principles, citizens have a right and obligation to act. Action may include mobilizing others, voting out of office officials who betray their oaths, or pursuing legal recourse. Too often elected officials who take an oath to defend the nation's principles do not themselves truly understand the substance and meaning of those principles.

Confidence in government is critical to maintain it. A "just society possesses a conscience, a sense of decency and humanity for all its citizens."[8] Decency involves respect and dignity, as well as a sense of community.

IGNORANCE FOSTERS INCIVILITY

A critical question facing the nation is: What are the odds of a democracy surviving if the citizens are not knowledgeable about government and its values, principles, and procedures? "Keeping" a democracy rests on an informed and participative electorate.

Citizens have a duty to make a commitment to become educated and knowledgeable. Living with the freedom of choice and opportunity politically and civically requires a principled commitment to do so. A complacent citizenry is a danger to its own aspirations and heritage.

Today, political conflict is rife in the media and newspapers, as well as in the public square and universities. Sharp opinions, some with little understanding or accuracy, are espoused, and scapegoating is becoming more prevalent. Freedom of speech and civility become issues.

Unfortunately, there are problems. The annual Annenberg Constitution Day Civics Survey[9] found that many Americans are poorly informed about basic constitutional knowledge. The study found that 37 percent of those surveyed could not name any of the rights under the First Amendment, and only 26 percent could name all three branches of the federal government.

In the survey, nearly 48 percent cited freedom of speech as a right guaranteed by the First Amendment, but an unprompted 37 percent could not name any other rights. Only 15 percent and 14 percent identified freedom of religion and freedom of the press, respectively.

In another study conducted by the National Center for Educational Statistics, two-thirds of eighth-graders did not know the historical importance of the Declaration of Independence.[10] Understanding government and the principles in the basic documents is vital knowledge for all citizens. They must make sense of proposals, political positions, Supreme Court decisions, and press and media reports. If they have no or limited knowledge of important documents and the principles stipulated in them, they will be inept in comprehending the impact and precedent.

The danger in democracy is clear. How can citizens protect their rights or the rights of others if they do not know what they are? Ignorance is not bliss when it comes to citizenship, governance, and politics. Education was meant to produce knowledgeable citizens. Eleanor Roosevelt stated, "Learning to be a good citizen is learning to live to the maximum of one's abilities and opportunities, and every subject should be taught with this view."[11]

In a Brookings Institute Survey, a plurality of college students (44 percent) do not believe that the US Constitution protects so-called hate speech, when in fact it does, as validated in the unanimous decision of *Matal v. Tam* by the Supreme Court. Free speech, while it may be offensive, is a basic principle. Curtailing speech beyond Supreme Court limitations is dangerous because it leaves open the appropriateness of speech to the fickle masses and people in power.

In a lecture, Bret Stephens, a *New York Times* journalist, stated, "In other words, to disagree well you must first understand well. You have to read deeply, listen carefully, and watch closely. You need to grant your adversary moral respect; give him the intellectual benefit of the doubt; have sympathy for his motives and participate empathically with his line of reasoning."[12]

In some cases today, individuals have been categorized and some shut down on university campuses. Stephens indicates that 51 percent of college students think it is acceptable to shout down a speaker with whom they disagree, and 20 percent agree that it is acceptable to use violence to prevent a speaker from presenting.

In essence, individuals use incivility to suppress comments that they feel arouse incivility. Quite ironic! The lack of understanding of the First Amendment results in those with good intentions and motives possibly destroying the system they wish to protect. The result in these circumstances is that others remain silent and do not express themselves, rather than risk being labeled negatively by others.

Silencing others is an authoritarian act with repercussions. American democracy is based on people having minds of their own, not marching in lockstep with power groups or advocating only socially accepted positions.

Not going along with the group and standing on principle, going against the grain and being an independent thinker, were part of American society and folklore. If this aim is thwarted, then a vacuum occurs: people withdraw and their opinions are silenced to conform to group pressures. Silencing opinions can create a misunderstanding of public opinion, and it raises concern about the accuracy of opinion polls, as the 2016 presidential election demonstrated.

Conforming means not standing out—individualism fades, along with its energy and creativity. Standing alone against the conformists has a righteous message and can inspire reflection and reconsideration. The conformer, to gain social acceptance, can lose not only identity but also the ability to act, which shifts responsibility to address issues to the group or collective.

Being a citizen sometimes means having the courage to go against the social or political grain. Courage, however, is not being free of fear. It requires overcoming it. Individuals acting on their own can influence an entire community if they are able to openly express their ideas.

EDUCATION FOR CIVIL CITIZENSHIP

Well-educated people require essential knowledge, understanding ideas, and developing the intellectual skills necessary to continue to learn and grow. America is based on ideas, and it takes more than factual recall to grasp, interpret, and apply them.

The old-fashioned three Rs (reading, writing, and arithmetic) are not obsolete because behind them are thinking skills. They are active, not passive pursuits, by students. Each in its own way demonstrates the quality of thought, the rational basis for their point of view, and the depth of understanding to express, defend, and refine proposals and positions.

Howard Gardner cited the Paideia proposal for education as a possible model: "Mastering disciplines, learning to communicate effectively, engaging civilly in discussion and argument—these have and should remain at the forefront of all education. The ancients talked about the importance of understanding what is true (and what is not); what is beautiful (and what is not worth lingering over); and what is good (in terms of being a worthy person, worker, and citizen). These educational goals should be perennial."[13]

The Paideia proposal[14] focuses on acquiring knowledge, developing intellectual skills, and understanding ideas and values. All children would be exposed to the same content knowledge, including language, literature, fine arts, mathematics, natural science, history, geography, and social studies. Reading, didactic presentations, and student responses are the means to gain knowledge.

Mastering skills and concepts in reading, writing, speaking, researching, mathematics, reasoning, problem solving, questioning, analyzing, synthesizing, and thinking provide a necessary foundation for children to become well educated. Questioning is an important method. Questions range from simple knowledge and recall to the more complex ones of analysis, synthesis, and evaluation. Higher-order questions require a depth of thinking to respond to them.

These essential skills enable children to learn the significant concepts that are the foundations for communication, mathematics, science, social science, and the arts. Concepts and ideas in these academic areas, however, are not discrete because they are vital in applying critical judgment. Seeing connections between and across content, concepts, and theories and being able to think critically and imaginatively about them are basic to citizenship and civil discussion.

Schools should fan the creative sparks in children because society needs innovative citizens. Historically, the standing of the United States, the American Dream, and economy and society rests on innovation, ingenuity, and the creativity of individuals. To flourish as a culture, children's innate imaginative heart must be nurtured and developed. The arts and other programs that encourage imaginative thinking have for too long been stepchildren in schools.

Socratic dialogue is an old but effective method of challenging students' thought processes and reasoning. Students must answer questions followed by subsequent questions that require them to analyze and assess their logic, reasoning, and understanding. These are basic skills of civility and citizenship. Socratic dialogue can also be used in discussions with public officials, policymakers, and others.

Socratic questioning and active participation leads to comprehension and understanding of ideas and values. Discussing books, political ideas (freedom and equality), and formal presentations spur understanding. These activities require students to confront ideas, assess them, and present them in a formal manner. Students of all ages can learn through discussion and seminars that are age appropriate.

CIVILITY IN SCHOOLS

Leadership in schools is critically important to establish and model civility. Superintendents, principals, and teachers all play vital roles in ensuring a culture and climate that is civil and proper in order to foster growth, learning, and creativity. Incivility is a destructive virus that shatters relationships and atmosphere, along with the entire school climate and culture.

All school personnel must model respect and appreciation for others—peers, students, and leaders. After all, the teaching and support staff are significant role models for students. Treating people well and recognizing their positive effort and outcomes verbally and in writing have a powerful impact on all.

Children and adults must be mindful and conscious of their impact on interactions and relationships. Put down the smartphone and look up at what is happening—be present. Self-monitoring for both staff and students is a skill that has rewards throughout life.

Another key factor is asking for feedback. How do people perceive the style and approaches in the school? Teachers can do this in the classroom with the entire class, as well as one on one with students through discussions or surveys.

Civil behavior should be reinforced positively. Within the professional team, a dialogue about concrete norms and expectations for civility and the behavior of students and others should be developed and monitored. Those who do not meet standards and who are uncivil should be confronted and disciplined appropriately to bring about positive change. Leaders must be aware of and monitor the emotions of teachers and students. Understanding the sources of individual behavior and assessing issues regularly will help evaluate the status of the school culture and climate so that improvements can be made.

Children take their emotional cues from the people around them. They must learn to self-regulate their behavior and understand its impact, as well as determine whether it meets acceptable norms. As adults, they must control and redirect negative emotions and impulses and be able to consider others' feelings and act in positive ways to reach their goals and desired outcomes.

Developing self-confidence, accepting constructive criticism, and acting in credible and trustworthy ways are necessary in all adult roles, including partisan politics and citizenship. Life brings ambiguity and change along with success and failure. Learning to manage relationships, work with others, and confront the best way to reach goals translate to adulthood and a civil society.

Daniel Goleman[15] identified five important components of emotional intelligence for children and adults that apply to civility. They include:

- *Self-awareness*: the ability to recognize and understand their moods, emotions, and their effect on others.
- *Self-regulation*: the ability to control and redirect eruptive impulses and moods and to suspend judgment and think before acting.
- *Motivation*: work for reasons that go beyond money or status and pursue goals with energy and persistence.
- *Empathy*: the ability to understand the emotional makeup of other people and skill in treating them according to their emotional reactions.
- *Social skill*: proficiency in managing relationships and building networks and ability to find common ground and build rapport.

Individuals with these abilities demonstrate self-confidence, are realistic in their self-assessments, and are trustworthy and behave with integrity. Optimism and sensitivity are key factors in their pursuit of goals. However, failure in most cases is the result of bad habits and destructive relationships. Poor decisions and irresponsible behavior curtail hopes and dreams. Children need positive examples and support through straight talk and accountability.

WHAT SCHOOLS CAN DO

Understanding that citizens' involvement requires agreeing to disagree on some issues and their impact is necessary. Things do not always go the way individuals desire. Democracies are not tensionless: they are vibrant and, at times, stirring, calling on people to show the passion of disagreement and celebrate the freedom to speak and debate openly and safely.

The National Council for the Social Studies[16] developed a position paper on creating effective citizens. The qualities of an effective citizen include:

- Embracing core democratic values and striving to live by them
- Accepting responsibility for the well-being of oneself, one's family, and the community
- Being knowledgeable of the people, history, and traditions that have shaped our local communities, our nation, and the world
- Understanding the nation's founding documents, civic institutions, and political processes
- Being aware of issues and events that have an impact on people at local, state, national, and global levels
- Seeking information from varied sources and perspectives to develop informed opinions and creative solutions
- Asking meaningful questions and being able to analyze and evaluate information and ideas
- Using effective decision-making and problem-solving skills in public and private life
- Collaborating effectively as a member of a group
- Participating actively in civic and community life

An educational program to produce capable citizens, according to the National Council for the Social Studies, ensures that:

- Civic knowledge, skills, and values are taught explicitly and systematically at every grade level.
- School and classroom management and culture exemplify and demonstrate core democratic values.
- Citizenship education is integrated throughout and across the curriculum.
- Students have meaningful opportunities to participate in class and school governance.
- All students at every grade level are provided with opportunities to participate in the civic life of their school and community.
- Learning activities extend beyond the school and invite parents and the community to participate and work with students.
- Students are provided with opportunities to participate in simulations, service-learning projects, conflict-resolution programs, and other activities that encourage the application of civic knowledge, skills, and values.

- All students are provided with instruction on our nation's founding documents, civic institutions, and political processes.
- All students are provided with instruction on the people, history, and traditions that have shaped our local communities, our nation, and the world.
- All students are explicitly recognized as an important part of the school mission.

In a 2017 summit titled *In a Democracy at a Crossroads*, a report was issued ("The Republic Is (Still) at Risk—and Civics Is a Part of the Solution"), and it specified six "proven practices" that can enhance children's civic learning. They include: (1) courses on civics, government, law, and related subjects; (2) deliberation on current, controversial issues; (3) service learning; (4) student-led voluntary associations; (5) student voice in schools; and (6) simulation of adult civic roles. [17]

WHAT DO CIVIL CITIZENS REQUIRE?

Preparing children for citizenship should be a priority because a democracy requires citizens who have the knowledge and thinking required to govern themselves and make authoritative decisions. Certainly, a broad liberal arts education prepares students for the future with its focus on ideas, values, and thinking.

Education must be dynamic and ongoing, with an understanding of the principles and values that form the foundation of the democracy but also still have relevance to an evolving future. In an unfolding world, creativity and the continuous intellectual curiosity to respond and shape the future are required. Understanding responsibilities in a democratic society and gaining some sense of historical perspective about duty to family, community, and country is a cornerstone to life in a democracy.

Education is about living fully with purpose and meaning and being an active and productive individual and citizen. Happiness is not pursued: it results from a life well lived that comes from within each person capitalizing on their uniqueness and following their heart, as well as their intellect.

In actuality, the real search for individuals is to discover who they are—their talents, passion, and path in life. Education has a spiritual dimension, not in a religious sense, but through grasping life's meaning and purpose, involving mindfulness and consciousness of the world, and relationships to others and to themselves. This entails self-understanding to authentically pursue those things that are in harmony with their heart and soul, as well as their mind and values.

The most difficult question to answer is "Who am I?" No standardized test can measure this, although, perversely, it can stymie the pursuit. The capacity to see with new eyes opens minds and perceptions about what is unfolding in the world with a fresh perspective. Being mindful and aware of the integration of issues and ideas and what is unfolding is important. Education should broaden children's perspectives, not narrow them.

To do so, children must be able to safely succeed and fail, discover their strengths and passions, and develop their character. Children also require the attitudes and values to persevere in the face of obstacles and complex problems. Trying and failing are a part of learning.

Learning from those failures and not losing their natural curiosity is indispensable for resilient people. They should discover their uniqueness and see the connections they have to the world, society, and others. A good education helps children discover what wants to emerge from within them: who they are and what their mission and purpose in life is.

Listening, perceiving, and understanding connections in life are important to continue to learn and adapt. An open mind and heart involves the intersection of understanding obligations to others and acting with integrity. Empathy, honesty, and compassion promote civility in both attitude and behavior.

In addition, stewardship and citizenship have the ethical obligation to do the "right" thing. Changing times require understanding the ethics and values that underpin our democracy and civil society. Strong ethical and moral frameworks are indispensable for wise decision making; otherwise, the common good dissolves, corruption blossoms, and tyranny takes root.

Children should grow to be wise as well as smart. Wisdom concerns "right" conduct in relation to others and to oneself. Unfortunately, in schools today, we seldom talk about wisdom.

WHAT CITIZENS MUST KNOW

- Citizens require an equal education. They need to comprehend the impact of the founding documents, the formation and duties of the branches of government, and the values that are the foundation of American government and culture.
- Civil deliberation requires understanding democracy with the requirements to sustain goodness, truth, liberty, justice, equality, and beauty.
- Civility requires understanding the similarities and differences between people.
- Deliberative discussions bring people together and do not include demonizing or disrespecting others. These discussions emphasize means, interests, and questioning.
- Silencing others from speaking is itself a nondemocratic and authoritarian act that creates divisions and risks suppression of others, including those who silence individuals.
- Citizens must master thinking and questioning skills and learn how to engage in civil discussions.
- Socratic dialogue is an approach that sharpens understanding of others' positions, as well as mastering one's own position.
- Teachers and others must model civility in schools and to learn to regulate themselves socially and personally.
- Education is not simply about preparation for employment. It is about preparation for life, meeting duties and responsibilities, and having a strong liberal arts education to understand self, society, history, creativity, and philosophy.

NOTES

1. Mortimer J. Adler, *The Paideia Proposal: An Educational Manifesto* (New York: Macmillan, 1982), 3.

2. Peter Levine and Kei Kawashima-Ginsberg, "The Republic Is (Still) at Risk—and Civics Is Part of the Solution," Jonathan M. Tisch College of Civic Life, Tufts University, 2017, http://www.civxsummit.org/documents/v1/SummitWhitePaper.pdf.

3. Meira Levinson, "Prepare Students to Be Citizens," *Phi Delta Kappan*, http://www.kappanonline.org/rd-prepare-students-citizens/.

4. James MacGregor Burns, *Transforming Leadership* (New York: Atlantic Monthly Press, 2003), 213.

5. Amitai Etzioni, *The New Rule: Community and Morality in a Democratic Society* (New York: Basic Books, 1996), 95–96.

6. Etzioni, *The New Rule*, 104.

7. Gary Hart, *The Republic of Conscience* (New York: Blue Rider Press, 2015), 128–29.

8. Hart, *The Republic of Conscience*, 130.

9. Annenberg Public Policy Center, "Americans Are Poorly Informed about Basic Constitutional Provisions," September 12, 2017, https://www.annenberg publicpolicycenter.org/americans-are-poorly-informed-about-basic-constitutional-provisions/.

10. Jon Schnur, "Can We Teach Kids to Be Good Citizens?" *Time*, December 6, 2011, http://Time.com/2011/12/06/can-we-teach-kids-to-be-good-citizens.

11. Eleanor Roosevelt, "Good Citizenship: The Purpose of Education," Eleanor Roosevelt Papers Project, George Washington University, https://www2.gwu.edu/~erpapers/documents/articles/goodcitizenship.cfm.

12. Bret Stephens, "The Dying Art of Disagreement," *New York Times*, September 24, 2017.

13. cmrubinworld.com, "Global Search for Education: Reimagining Learning on July 4 with Dr. Howard Gardner," 2017.

14. Adler, *The Paideia Proposal*, 23.

15. Daniel Goleman, "What Makes a Leader?" *Harvard Business Review* (2015): 6.

16. National Council for the Social Studies, 2013, http://www.socialstudies.org/sites/default/files/publications/se/6505/650511.html.

17. Levine and Kawashima-Ginsberg, "The Republic Is (Still) at Risk."

10

THINKING AND CIVIL DIALOGUE

Every child in America should be acquainted with his own country. He should read books that furnish him with ideas that will be useful to him in life and practice. As soon as he opens his lips, he should rehearse the history of his own country.
—Noah Webster, *On the Education of Youth in America*, 1788

Democratic societies have an oxymoronic nature: the very freedoms and protections that unite citizens make conflict inevitable. However, it is the right kind of conflict if it is civil, respects the rights of others, and presents ideas and challenges to ensure the integrity of those freedoms. American society does not speak with one voice. Factions emerge and movements arise.

According to Bill Bishop, a "Big Sort" has been occurring in the United States over the past forty years. He states that the "Big Sort" "is not simply about political partisanship, about how Americans vote every couple of years. It is a division in what they value, in how they worship, and in what they expect out of life."[1] The result is growing separation and intolerance, making consensus very difficult.

The "Big Sort" is occurring for multiple reasons besides politics. For example, educational attainment is an unexpected factor: highly educated liberals and conservatives become more liberal or conservative and congregate with those of like mind. In addition, individuals with higher educations are more mobile geographically and socially—roots are not as deep. Geographic location, both rural and urban, also creates division, as the judgments and characterizations of the media and others label people negatively.

Americans disassociate from individuals they see as different and, instead, surround themselves with reassuring media and "friends." They read, listen, and watch news and media that is in harmony with their philosophical disposition. This creates a vacuum of emptiness and little or no interaction with others.

A problem with sorting of this nature is that "like-minded, homogeneous groups squelch dissent, grow more extreme in their thinking, and ignore evidence that their positions are wrong. As a result, we now live in a giant feedback loop, hearing our own thoughts about what's right and wrong bounce back to us by the television shows we watch, the newspapers and books we read, the blogs we visit online, the sermons we hear, and the neighborhoods we live in."[2]

People tend to categorize others not part of their group quite simplistically into "good" or "bad" categories. Little refinement or complexity goes into those choices. Many times, groups are considered "with us" or "against us" without any real evidence or depth of understanding of their positions.

Consequently, individuals develop strategies and coalitions to beat or defeat groups or individuals with whom they disagree. In these circumstances, conversations or discussions never take place or become extremely difficult because mistrust destroys any possibility of connection.

ENEMYFYING

Adam Kahane coined a word, *enemyfy*, to describe what individuals do in these circumstances. *Enemyfying* is "thinking and acting as if the people we are dealing with are our enemies—people who are the cause of our problems and hurting us."[3] In other situations, people might use different words that are softer and not as divisive: *rivals, competitors, opponents,* or *adversaries*.

Enemies connote a very harsh view. People may want to defeat opponents and rivals, but with enemies, their nature is to destroy them. Winning becomes a matter of blaming others for conditions and labeling them as threats to people's way of life, security, or safety. They say things like

"Those people are the reason things are messed up and why our security is at risk."

The conflict on some college campuses concerning speech goes to levels of enemyfying—speakers and others are portrayed as hostile enemies of society and culture tagged with an epithet of some left or right skew.

Enemyfying others can feel righteous and even heroic. There is little intention of problem solving, and certainly no collaboration. When fragmentation of this nature moves beyond labels, civility evaporates and vitriol increases, which can threaten people and property.

Enemyfying can be arrogant and comforting because it reassures those who categorize others that they are not responsible for the issues or difficulties. Citing and stamping others as enemies is quite simple: "We are right, they are wrong" or "We are moral, they are not." However, there is a problem.

Complex issues usually do not have simple solutions, nor are one-dimensional analyses the answer. In addition, there is a matter of constitutional rights and people's right to free speech even if it is foolish, wrong, or irritating.

Enemyfying obscures issues and contexts as well as distorts the challenges society faces. Verbal rock throwing actually destroys diversity—the diversity of thought and ideas—and thwarts any conversation or dialogue with others. Diversity is more than ethnicity, race, and other demographics. It also concerns thoughts and opinions and ideas and interpretations.

Polarization and seeking like-mindedness increases through enemyfying, which limits conversation and results in greater isolation. Alienation is a corrupting influence and a deterrent to finding areas of agreement, if any, or simply understanding the principles and attitudes of others.

Enemyfying is not strictly a conservative or liberal, or a Republican or Democrat, position. It is evident and practiced in both parties, as well as corporate and other private or public sector venues.

People resort to enemyfying because they have not truly developed a position or cannot make their own case. Individuals frequently apply it if they do not have a thorough understanding of issues or cannot state their position articulately. It is easier to simply lash out at others than review and research their positions.

Disagreement is not enemyfying. It is a natural and even desired response when discussion of decisions and options are on the table. It can clarify positions and open the door to new or revised positions. Compassion and empathy, even if agreement is not present, can lead, at least, to greater understanding of other individuals' viewpoints and positions. Understanding why people think and feel the way they do increases tolerance.

FRAMING CIVIL ARGUMENTS

In all facets of life there are decisions, various points of view, and debate about circumstances and philosophies. Presenting a point of view and entering the debate is a duty of citizenship. The question is: How can citizens present their views effectively and civilly?

In situations in which countervailing positions are presented, trust is a major factor and objective, which can be undone through incivility, misrepresentations, or false information. Opinions or positions may be wrong, but being deceitful and untrustworthy is intolerable.

The late Supreme Court justice Antonin Scalia discussed how to present a case and the importance of trust in the process: "Trust is won by fairly presenting the facts of the case and honestly characterizing the issues; by owning up to those points that cut against you and addressing them forthrightly; and by showing respect for the intelligence of your audience."[4] His advice pertains not only to the courtroom but also to public and personal discussion.

Sometimes people fail to tell the whole truth, use selective facts and examples, and denigrate those with whom they disagree. In these cases, believability and credibility are lost even with those who may be sympathetic to the prospective position. Honesty is a very basic principle in presenting ideas in informal discussions or formal circumstances politically or professionally.

Logic and rational reasoning are powerful foundations in presenting the truth in moral, academic, and legal arguments. Students need to learn to use logic and rational discourse in presenting positions and alternatives.

Practicing making a case can be done in every academic classroom. In many cases, students have positions on school practice and policy and other matters and are willing to engage. Learning to make a case is more than arguing in the vernacular. Blasting or ridiculing each other is not making the argument.

Emotional appeals can be powerful, but they are best used when substantiated by reason, logic, and facts. Visceral connections are powerful only if they withstand logical and factual assessment. In many cases, emotional approaches can be seen as manipulative and without reason or foundation. Presenting ethically and logically creates the basis for finding solutions.

Several factors are important in presenting viewpoints or debating issues. The first, beyond presenting in an ethical fashion, is to know your audience and their position on the matter at hand. Without that understanding, the nature of the presentation, the language used, and the detail involved can be either off-putting or insulting to the audience.

Scalia indicates that being "scrupulously accurate"[5] is absolutely necessary. Don't state or make statements that are overblown or incorrect. Careless or loose use of factual information destroys credibility—the major quality people have in any discussion or debate.

Trying to defend the indefensible destroys reasoning and the rationale that is basic to maintain a position. This applies to the argument as well as the opposition. Reasonableness and good judgment require recognizing the positions of others and seeing the validity of some positions they may hold. Outlandish characterizations or positions destroy any authority the speaker may have.

In making an argument, major positions are presented followed by specific facts, which help others understand the basis for the argument, along with supporting evidence and circumstances. Rambling through a discussion or debate creates impatience and frustration, as others wish to "just get to the point!" Emotional screeching and bombast highlights irrationality, and does not garner support.

All students must think clearly and have strong language skills to communicate distinctly and concisely. Almost everyone has experienced individuals who ramble on and on or act as blowhards. They destroy their own argument through self-inflicted wounds and arrogance.

Finally, common sense is a forceful way to present ideas. Respecting the arguments of others in a civil manner is important. Disrespect does not unite or convince. Arrogance is repulsive. Moral superiority demonstrates shallowness, and judgmentalism turns people away. Accusatory statements and overemotional tirades destroy any possibility of others listening and accepting an individual's ideas or rationale.

Students must master their position and points of view to be able to be self-expressive and respected citizens. All of these components of debate help individuals understand the cognitive and emotional foundations for their viewpoints. From this, the possibility of listening actively to others in order to comprehend their position increases.

Several strategies are helpful in having constructive discussions.[6] Students should understand and practice them in the classroom and school. They include the ability to:

- Balance emotion with reason—curtailing irrationality
- Understand and have empathy for others in the discussion
- Inquire, consult, and listen, which leads to better two-way communication and creates a genuine interest in others
- Create a foundation of trust and confidence
- Openness to persuasion; persuasion is more powerful in the long term than coercion
- Accept others as worthy—deal with people with an open and civil mind

The success of America rests on the ability of citizens to participate effectively and positively with the interchange of ideas. Problem solving involves a broad perspective across content and a deep understanding of the principles and moral expectations to create and maintain a civil society. Comprehending cultural values and their philosophical foundations are necessary for ethical and moral decision making and conduct.

THINKING

Educated people are skeptics, not cynics or sheep. They ask questions and try to discern the truth. They see through distortions, self-interest, and unethical use of data and information. Being skeptical is fundamental in being a critical thinker and an active family member, employee, and citizen.

Skepticism applies reason to critical thinking to determine whether arguments, assumptions, or proposals are valid. It is absolutely essential to be applied in order to expose "junk" thought and other forms of deception. In this political age, cynicism is not needed, but skepticism is. "Critical thinking is skeptical without being cynical. It is open-minded without being wishy-washy. It is analytical without being nitpicking."[7]

The term *skeptic* is derived from the Greek word *skeptikos*, meaning "to inquire, to look around." Skeptics examine information, analyze it, and possibly require more particulars and data to determine whether proposals or commentaries are true. They just don't accept data or documentation because it is presented authoritatively in articles or media. Voters need these skills and dispositions, actually, before casting a ballot, asking, "Is this really true, accurate, and plausible?"

The ability to comprehend, analyze, and evaluate ideas, propositions, and proposals is necessary in private life as well as socially and politically. Reviewing and processing information, making connections to issues and situations, and creating new perspectives are needed in solving problems, defining options, and making decisions. Challenging options requires sharp cognitive skills and the ability to analyze and determine the accuracy and reasonableness of propositions.

Analytical thinking and problem solving go hand in hand in determining the issues and factors underlying them. Logical analyses and problem definition require bringing facts and information together and determining viability. Separating desires from reality is essential. Emotion can curtail rational analysis.

Generating solutions is a matter of exploring factors involved in the issue and the ability to understand the essential aspects of the problem or concern. Subtleties exist and sometimes carry more influence and power than the obvious tangibles. Conflict, problems, and issues are opportunities to think creatively and find options and innovative results.

Well-informed citizens are able to critically reflect on issues of the day. Gullible citizens are an anathema to a democracy. Being contemplative and rational is of critical importance as access to ideas, information, and opinions are just a click away.

Peter A. Facione, in his essay "Critical Thinking: What It Is and Why It Counts,"[8] identifies the key components of critical thinking. They include:

- *Interpretation*: the ability to understand the information presented, its meaning, and significance.

- *Analysis*: the ability to connect pieces of information, statements, concepts, and descriptions and to determine what the meaning of the information represents.
- *Inference*: the ability to understand specifics and what is needed to determine an accurate conclusion from the information. Are the conclusions reasonable?
- *Evaluation*: the ability to evaluate the credibility of statements, judgments, or opinions to determine the validity of the information presented.
- *Explanation*: the ability to restate information and add clarity and perspectives so others can understand it and to state the reasoning—concepts, context, methods—upon which the results were based.
- *Self-regulation*: having an awareness of one's own reasoning and thinking used to find results and to monitor one's own cognitive activities and judgments.

Without skeptical and critical thinking, democracy could fall victim to authoritarianism and the collapse of institutions upon which democracy depends. A liberal education is about learning to learn: to think for one-self and not accept the disposition and dominance of authority. A concern for principle and integrity and the common good brings reasoned and rational deliberation and action.

ACTIVE LISTENING AND DIALOGUE

Education provides the tools to engage responsibly and productively with people who are agreeable or disagreeable to one's own views. There are processes and tools all children should learn.

A primary skill is listening. Too often individuals try to overpower others by shouting, talking over, cutting them off, or formulating responses before they complete their sentences. They are thinking of their response before the other person finishes their point.

Active listening is more than sitting silently. It presumes that the other person has something to offer. According to Fred Kofman,[9] a major goal is exploring each other's reasoning and understanding what they think and why.

As part of the discussion, comprehending the impact of one's comments or actions on others is important. In essence, learning the other person's story and perspective is beneficial in finding areas of emphasis and different interpretations that create deeper understanding. On the other side of the ledger, expressing individual thoughts and feelings helps others understand another's perspective. In each case, clarity, honesty, and respect must be evident—they must go both ways.

When understanding is attained, addressing circumstances together can begin. Each individual learns something about the other. "Given what you and the other person have each learned, what would improve the situation going forward?"[10] It is a critical question, and a necessary one in order to make progress. Hopefully, a respectful context for conversation can be created. Finding common purpose based on mutual respect is at the core of understanding.

Kofman indicates that finding common ground and making an "I" statement expressing one's position and feelings are unifying actions. Individuals should stay away from "you" statements that paint the other person as the nemesis or problem. Major issues necessitate comprehending and understanding each other. Getting feedback and being open to receiving it is a positive aspect of communication. To converse, individuals must stay open, be quiet and not interrupt, and listen to the person's feelings and position. It is helpful to summarize when the person is finished and check for accurate understanding.

Two things are very important with active listening. One is to understand the content of messages—the communication itself. Second, comprehend the intent of the communication. "In active listing you clarify the content and intent of messages in a nonjudgmental manner. Simply saying 'I hear you say that you are frustrated with . . .' or 'I sense that you are angry about . . .' and listening to the response can make a big difference in promoting understanding and letting the person know you are interested and comprehend his or her full meaning."[11]

Many times, a group has to tackle a difficult issue with individuals coming from a variety of viewpoints and some of them contrary and conflicting. With complex issues facing organizations in the country, dialogue can be a constructive way to come together, define the issues, and find areas of agreement and move ahead, without fragmenting into subgroups and subcultures.

DIALOGUE

Dialogue is necessary for effective group action. Active listening certainly plays a critical role in this process and helps identify issues. Dialogue focuses primarily on the thinking process: what the group thinks collectively so that shared meanings and clear thinking are defined.

William Isaacs defined dialogue as "shared inquiry, a way of thinking and reflecting together. It is not something you do *to* a person. It is something you do *with* another person."[12] The intention of dialogue is not to take sides but to reach a new understanding and find a fresh foundation from which to think and act.

Isaacs believes dialogue is a conversation not with sides but with a center. Channeling the energy of differences to come to a new understanding and formulate the ability to think anew is the goal. Linking together to listen deeply to each other and inquiry into the possibility of something new unfolding can be the result.

Actually, dialogue is a means to think together by suspending judgment and certainty. Listening is very important in this process, as individuals speak their own truth (voicing). Listening without resistance or judgment is imperative, along with respecting the integrity of another's perspective. Too often people cannot let go of their judgments and believe what they think is without question.

Dialogue opens three doors: the good, the true, and the beautiful.[13] The good concerns morals and collective action, the true is the pursuit of objective truth, and the beautiful focuses on aesthetics, the heart, and morals. Hopefully, dialogue enables participants to overcome fragmentation through this common inquiry.

Today the irony is that with technology people can be connected—in touch, not isolated—but Isaacs asserts that while technology provides connection, it does not make contact, which means sharing understanding, insight, wisdom, or matters of the heart. Discerning content and intent are quite difficult to comprehend online, along with feeling the passion and energy of the other person.

Dialogue causes reflection and the capacity to suspend judgment and let go of old memories and judgments. Individuals speak in a way that seeks to contribute to one another and not simply by extracting things from one another.

Developing a shared meeting is the goal of dialogue between disparate groups. Hierarchy is not a part of the dialogue process and, hopefully, a form of collective leadership arises. A "free flow of meaning"[14] emerges, and people respect each other and the process so that creativity can surface as people speak together openly and consciously. They just do not present stock answers or platitudes.

Confronting and understanding one's own personal assumptions and those of others, along with the feelings behind them, can lead to building common ground. From this point as a group, shared assumptions can be identified and a common understanding can be constructed. Collaboration can occur to find solutions and resolution to issues, problems, or conflict.

Adam Kahane[15] proposes a process that "stretches" collaboration because harmony, certainty, and compliance cannot always be achieved with conventional dialogue. He proposes an enhanced dialogue process.

Understanding that, in collaboration, it is inevitable that people must work with individuals with whom they do not agree or like, Kahane believes that embracing conflict in connection with others is necessary. Instead of insisting on clear agreement concerning the problems or solutions, the group should move to experimenting systematically with different perspectives and possibilities. Finally, he states that rather than trying to change what others are doing, individuals must move ahead actively and be open to the prospect of even changing themselves.

Obviously, getting things accomplished with others and their diverse perspectives is not easy. Complexities arise, and individuals must move ahead and not be fearful or reticent. They must approach issues with more awareness. Sometimes individuals must see and acknowledge their own role and responsibility for the issues—even, at times, sacrificing what is familiar or what they desire.

Kahane promotes stretch collaboration, which involves three basic shifts. First, individuals must embrace conflict using two drives. One is a drive for self-regulation and asserting oneself. The other is a desire for reunification by engaging others. Both of these drives are essential.

Second, individuals must be open, talking and especially listening, to help new positions to emerge rather than simply regurgitating their individual positions and debating, which reinforces the status quo.

Finally, becoming involved requires the possibility of changing oneself and not remaining above the action by only attempting to change other people. Dialoguing requires a sense of curiosity and openness, as well as being self-reflective. Working in dialogue with people with whom you disagree requires engagement, not labeling or disputing.

CONCLUSION

Several means of discourse are available. Telling is not the only approach. It is a typical behavior of experts, fundamentalists, autocrats, and those who are arrogant, angry, or afraid.

A second way of talking and listening is debating, which is a clash of ideas, with each person asserting views and opinions. In this case, there may be winners and losers.

Dialoguing is a third way of talking and listening. Listening to others, empathetically and subjectively, is demonstrated so that there is awareness of where the other individuals are coming from. The conversation becomes self-reflective and can open new possibilities.

Finally, a fourth way of talking and listening is "presencing,"[16] which is sensing what is coming into being and being fully present without any distraction in the conversation. Letting go of nonessentials and suspending habitual ways of operating can open new horizons. Old patterns dissolve. Sometimes sitting in silence together contemplating and feeling what wants to emerge is powerful. Being together without judgment but with understanding can lead to neutral connection. The boundaries between people disappear, and they become deeply engaged together as a group.

Too often individuals let their gut feelings overwhelm their reasoning, making it very difficult to listen or connect with others. Demands or emotional tirades are not productive in any democratic context.

A broad education includes content, skills, and thinking but also, hopefully, creating a path to wisdom. As Einstein said, "Any fool can know. The point is to understand."

WHAT CITIZENS MUST KNOW

• The "Big Sort" is about more than partisan politics. Divisions extend to education, philosophy, income, religion, and other factors.

- *Enemyfying* is thinking and acting as if people were enemies, beyond perceiving them as rivals. This pushes people to more extreme behavior in responding to those categorized in that manner.
- Citizens must learn how to frame arguments to present their views effectively.
- Logic and reasoning are powerful in framing positions as well as presenting them honestly and ethically and gaining trust.
- Respecting the arguments of others and creating a sense of trust is part of civil debate and discourse and important for acting with integrity.
- Citizens must be able to think skeptically and critically in reviewing options and solutions (and particularly in making decisions).
- Dialogue is a skill that is important in engaging in shared inquiry with others and in finding alternative solutions to questions.
- Active listening is necessary to understand the content and intent of individuals' comments, content, and messages.
- Listening, dialogue, and being self-reflective are necessary for a civil and respectful interchange.

NOTES

1. Bill Bishop, *The Big Sort: Why the Clustering of Like-Minded America Is Tearing Us Apart* (New York: Houghton Mifflin Harcourt, 2009), 13.

2. Bishop, *The Big Sort*, 38–39.

3. Adam Kahane, *Collaborating with the Enemy: How to Work with People You Don't Agree with or Like or Trust* (New York: Barrett-Koehler, 2017), 7.

4. Antonin Scalia and Bryan A. Garner, *Making Your Case* (St. Paul, MN: Thompson/West, 2008).

5. Scalia and Garner, *Making Your Case*.

6. Roger Fisher and Scott Brown, *Getting Together: Building Relationships as We Negotiate* (New York: Benjamin Publishing Group, 1989), 39–40.

7. Fisher and Brown, *Getting Together*, 23.

8. Peter A. Facione, "Critical Thinking: What It Is and Why It Counts," 2013, https://www.nyack.edu/files/CT_What_Why_2013.pdf.

9. Fred Kofman, *Authentic Communication: Transforming Conversation in the Workplace* (Boulder, CO: Sounds True, 2014).

10. Kofman, *Authentic Communication*.

11. George A. Goens, *Soft Leadership for Hard Times* (Lanham, MD: Rowman & Littlefield, 2005), 89–90.

12. William Isaacs, *Dialogue and the Art of Thinking Together* (New York: Currency Publishers, 1999), 9.

13. Isaacs, *Dialogue and the Art of Thinking Together*, 386.

14. Isaacs, *Dialogue and the Art of Thinking Together*, 395.

15. Kahane, *Collaborating with the Enemy*, 205.

16. Otto C. Scharmer, *Theory U* (Cambridge, MA: Society for Organizational Learning, 2007), 183–87.

11

KNOWLEDGEABLE AND WISE CITIZENSHIP

If we ask ourselves what is this wisdom which experience forces upon us, the answer must be that we discover the world is not constituted as we had supposed it to be. It is not that we learn more about its physical elements, or its geography, or the variety of its inhabitants, or the ways in which human society is governed. Knowledge of this sort can be taught to a child without in any way disturbing his childishness. . . . The essential discovery of maturity has little if anything to do with information about the names, the locations, and the sequence of facts; it is the acquiring of a different sense of life, a different kind of intuition about the nature of things.

—Walter Lippman

Excellence is never an accident. It is always the result of heightened tension, sincere effort, and intelligent execution; it represents the wise choice of many alternatives—choice, not chance, determines your destiny.

—Aristotle

Civility does not restrain the expression of ideas: it simply involves the manner in which ideas or proposals are conveyed. Name-calling, innuendo, or verbal barrages simply provoke abrasiveness and disrespect, creating total rejection not just of ideas but also of individuals and their positions.

Incivility raises ethical questions of how people treat each other. Disagreeing is not the question: it is part of a democracy, but the manner in which individuals challenge others does matter. Humiliating others or crass and vulgar "putdowns" eventually results in harassment, violence, or injury—all of which have no moral basis. Any politeness or awareness evaporates in egotistical arrogance, which is void of any understanding of others.

Oppressing and bullying others, even in defending virtuous principles, raises questions of character in addition to ethics. Being a good citizen requires being a civil citizen in discourse and behavior, even when it is not convenient or easy. "We can't speak about ethics and moral behaviors without talking about community, issues of morality exposed by human need, and the moral role that civility plays in the leadership culture."[1]

VIRTUE AND DISCIPLINE

Schools must address civility in words and actions. A fundamental question is how individuals treat each other properly in all circumstances whether as a peer or as a leader.

In essence, civility is about treating others as you would like to be treated: in short, the Golden Rule. Listening and building trust demonstrates respect for others and their dignity. Agreeing with others is not a requirement for civility. How disagreement takes place, however, is important for all concerned if true communication is ever going to occur.

Disgust is not the answer—eye rolling or hollering generates breaches, some of which will be difficult to ever repair. Disrespect closes doors and builds walls of resentment and hostility. Email counterattacks are damaging and raise negative reprisals and create continuing cycles of condemnation.

Citizenship requires reasoned discourse and arguments made on the merits of the case. Facts, examples, research, and logic are the means to determine not only areas of discord but also areas of agreement and possible compromise. In some cases, these discussions can open new possibilities and perspectives—spaces for connections and answers.

At times, matters of principle and its interpretation may continue the disagreement, but in a courteous, considerate, and respectful manner. Agreeing to disagree is a viable option and can raise the possibility of further discussions and the prospect of respectful friendship even though disagreement continues. At times, individuals who disagree over philosophy or the analysis of issues become great friends with deep regard and affection. But that only comes when both parties really listen to each other.

All citizens must be accepted for expressing their freedom and to engage even if their viewpoints, interpretations, and philosophies are revolting. Ad hominem attacks and resultant fractured relationships make coming together difficult, if not impossible. Civility is necessary in order for anyone to fulfill the potential of his or her life, work, or family, and it is basic to having a democracy by the people.

SCHOOLS AND VIRTUES

People are complex human beings with imaginations, moral standing, and personalities beyond measurement. Human beings are not always rational, and behavior cannot be easily measured metrically. The focus on metrics and data miss the fact that children are people who cannot be defined simply by test results or other metrics.

What is the metric for civility or compassion or character? Is there a metric for goodness, beauty, truth, justice, equality, or liberty? Ideas and concepts are not easily assessed by simple statistics collectively or individually.

"In actuality, the intangibles—principles, values, and ethics—that we desire in schools are the foundation for its integrity and credibility and ultimately effectiveness. Schools as sanctuaries for children provide high levels of care, compassion, and patience as students work their way to maturity. Actually, helping and encouraging children to find meaning and fulfillment is an act of love—not a technical quantitative exercise."[2]

Virtues are in the same category. They are concerned with behavior and character that have a moral sense to it. Americans value the character traits of honesty, compassion, and courage. Schools must model character if they expect to enforce self-discipline and civil conduct in students. Modeling civil behavior is important: children and students watch to see whether words and action are congruent.

When individuals slide off the rails and fail to control their temper and impulses, problems arise socially and personally. Self-discipline is important in all relationships, including citizenship. In addition, it is an expectation that individuals are disciplined to follow and respect the law. Learning and exhibiting self-control and respect for others are necessary to become a productive and respected citizen.

Students have responsibilities beyond themselves. Concepts like duty and honor seem out of touch today, particularly in social media, where self-centeredness is prevalent in "likes" and "selfies." However, these principles are important in families and neighborhoods.

Individuals acting with integrity and meeting their duty to others and themselves create a civil society. Acting with integrity is not without conflict or criticism. Raising issues and taking a position when things are out of skew requires courage. Silence in times when ethical and moral imperatives are jeopardized is dangerous. Indifference is a rebuke of citizenship itself.

At the heart of positive and productive attitudes and behavior are virtues. Children are keen observers of adult behavior. They are taught by the example of parents, relatives, public figures, and teachers. Unfortunately, public examples of political and entertainment figures are contrary, at times, to individuals of character and courage. Espousing one thing and doing another are examples of hypocritical and destructive behavior. Principles cannot be applied selectively or arbitrarily, and lip service is hypocritical.

The virtues that children need to study integral to good character and civility include[3]:

- *Self-discipline*: using good sense and judgment and taking charge of one's attitude, behavior, and performance.
- *Compassion*: taking the lives and emotions of others seriously and being supportive in good and difficult times.
- *Responsibility*: being accountable and answerable for behavior and actions.
- *Friendship*: loyalty, frankness, and assistance in a mutual friendship.
- *Hard work*: investing in activities and having pride in doing things well.
- *Courage*: standing ground on the basis of principle and ethics—doing the right thing and knowing what the right thing to do is.
- *Perseverance*: continuing and persisting by leading or empowering oneself for a worthy and just cause.

- *Honesty*: being real, genuine, and authentic in relationships and actions—being genuine with others.
- *Loyalty*: constancy of and steadfastness in attachments with other persons, groups, or ideals, which shows itself most clearly in times of stress.

Children must move out of their "me" mindset and understand that their decisions affect others. They must realize that being successful is more than being smart and intelligent. Life demands care and understanding of others. Character matters. And, in many situations, it has a bigger impact than brainpower alone. In the final analysis, life is about relationships with self, others, and community.

Ethical or moral conduct, with integrity to values and principles, is a responsibility of all citizens. The courage to act on them is necessary in all relationships.

Good intentions are not sufficient: behavior matters. Being a "good person begins with being a wise person. Then when you follow your conscience you'll be heading in the right direction."[4]

Living a life of explicit virtues and standards results in a life of moral integrity. "Duties and virtues are the focus for children to make decisions, act to help others, and develop their abilities and contribute beyond their own self-interest. In doing so, children must consider the following questions. What kind of person should I be or try to be? What are my obligations in the situation and what are the things I should never do?"[5] Integrity is a fundamental aspect of civility and treating people with dignity and respect.

An education is more than accumulating knowledge. An educated and cultured society can fall victim to heartless regimes and brutalizing terror and degradation. Without character, individuals and countries descend into unethical and diabolical motives and conduct.

WISDOM

Wisdom has internal and external contexts. It is usually defined through external actions or achievements. In reality, however, it begins within. Individuals with a sense of wisdom understand themselves. They recognize their own vulnerabilities and are comfortable in facing them. They do not see them as weaknesses but understand how to face the world and its contradictions because of them. They do not become artificial or disingenuous because of them.

Wisdom is rooted in strong values and the pursuit of truth and moral and principled outcomes in the best interests of individuals and society. While it requires knowledge, the foundation is based on virtue, a strong moral compass, and ethics.

When people think of wisdom, the stereotypical picture of a graying old person offering advice and counsel comes to mind, along with historical sages and philosophers, the assumption being that wisdom comes only with age or through exceptional intellect.

Wisdom is not synonymous with academics or IQ. It does not emanate simply from a regurgitation of facts or research. Wisdom involves more than intellect and content knowledge: highly intelligent people can do heinous things thoroughly absent of moral principles and human compassion. At times, people kowtow to those who are intelligent and cite research, propositions, and philosophy. However, people can be smart but not wise, and their influence and decisions can be catastrophic.

Parents, however, want their children to make wise decisions and to be responsible. Citizens have a voice in governing themselves, and that voice must be informed and wise, which requires not only knowledge but also moral and ethical foundations and application.

Moral imperatives, ethics, and principles provide the insight into what really matters and what ultimately is inconsequential. Wise people see connections beyond fragmented knowledge: they understand the interconnectedness of economics, politics, ethics, science, and art. They fulfill their obligations and act beyond self-interest to do what is right to enhance the development of a cultured society exemplified by a sense of "goodness."

Wisdom includes emotional and intellectual qualities. George Vaillant[6] specifies the qualities of wisdom to include the maturity to empathize with groups beyond their own, apply moral judgment and common sense, appreciate context, apply intelligence to discern core issues, and display the emotional intelligence of care and justice. In other words, wisdom is a product of the intellect and the heart.

Wisdom requires the intelligent application of knowledge and principles coupled with the insight of ethics and virtue. Values are essential in using knowledge for the "good" of people and society. Conscience is a barking dog when individuals act selfishly and without regard for their scruples and inner voice. Selfishness or arrogance deactivates individuals' moral compasses, creating rash or egocentric decisions.

Issues are complex and come with complications. Many times, there are no clear or easy answers—just a fog complete with fragmented information, speculative perspectives, and unknown and unpredictable forces.

Wisdom is required when information is lacking and unknowns and uncertainties obscure clarity. Abstract issues, as well as philosophical, practical, and spiritual ones, require judgment and understanding of the human condition and a means to plan and manage situations.

A sense about the conditions of life and human affairs is necessary. Good judgment is more than mastery of facts or information. Applying knowledge in a principled way is at the core of wise analysis, determining options, and making decisions for the good of the individual and others. "Wise people discern the inner qualities and essentials of relationships and are astute enough to see the subtle nuances of the impact of knowledge on people, relationships, and society. They are able to weld knowledge with compassion, integrity, imagination and hope."[7]

Wisdom is multifaceted, involving problem solving, managing social and other situations, introspection, and advice and counsel. A concern for matters of the heart as well as mind moves beyond knowing to understanding virtue and honor. Reasoning, patience, resilience, mindfulness, humility, and compassion are needed. Acknowledging uncertainty is a positive attribute along with being comfortable with conditions that require flexibility.

Being reflective and not jumping to conclusions or knee-jerk propositions is characteristic of reflection, leading to seeing the truth and circumstances. Insight defines both the subtle and the obvious meaning of situations and significance of situations. Grasping the human element—the intangibles of human nature—can lead to a comprehensive understanding of actions, issues, and impacts.

Hardship is going to exist. The truthful application of knowledge, comprehending what is unknown, and grappling with uncertainty is part of life personally and in all roles. Applying knowledge and acting wisely should bring benefit to everyone, even though, at times, it is not recognized.

ETHICAL APPROACHES

The late Antonin Scalia cautioned, "Modern man—perhaps mesmerized by the phenomenon of constant progress in the physical sciences—tends to think that constant progress in morality and ethics is also inevitable. That education will inevitably produce virtue, and every day in every way we will get better and better."[8]

In order for progress to be made in creating a caring and virtuous society, students must consider ethics. In all areas of study, actually—from science, history, political science, technology, law, the arts, and others—ethical questions arise. Matters of goodness are a concern in every home, as well as society. National questions and the behavior of the government and its officials must come under the scrutiny of ethics for the greater good.

Every citizen or policymaker at some time or another must consider substantial issues and concerns in their personal or public lives. Several approaches to ethical decision making are available.[9] Each offers a perspective that addresses decisions and the emphasis and impact.

The "utilitarian approach" basically boils down to providing the greatest good for the greatest number. Making a decision requires identifying the courses of action available, determining who is affected by each option, and then choosing the one that has the greatest benefits and the least harm.

Another ethical approach is the "rights approach" premised on the fact that "people have dignity based on their ability to choose freely what they will do with their lives, and they have a fundamental moral right to have those choices respected." Other associated rights are truth, privacy, safety, and equality. A determining question is: Does the action respect the moral rights of everyone?

A third ethical framework is the "virtue approach" based on the concept that there are ideals worth striving for. These ideals should help people act in ways that enable them to reach their highest potential. "Honesty, courage, compassion, generosity, fidelity, integrity, fairness, self-control, and prudence are examples." Benefits and burdens should be distributed fairly. Consistency of treatment of people is just—unless there are morally relevant differences between them.

Finally, the "common good approach" links an individual's own good to the good of the greater community, which is bound by the pursuit of common goals and values. There are conditions that are of consequence to everyone's advantage. This ethical approach focuses on social policies, social systems, environments, and institutions on which everyone depends and which are of benefit to all.

The common good approach moves to a larger sphere. The freedom of people to pursue their interests and goals is respected and valued. This approach challenges individuals and recognizes that policies, systems, and environments benefit all. Individuals are not isolated beings; they are members of a community and bound together. Hence the common good is important.

All of these ethical approaches bring important concepts to the fore. In relations with individuals or in examining public policy issues, these questions surface and should be discussed and considered. Understanding ethical thinking and dispositions can generate conversation and dialogue in a constructive and civil manner, focusing on reason, values, and ethics. Being able to understand the ethical impact of issues is fundamental. Having individuals reason together and understand issues from a different perspective can curtail instability and fragmentation.

America is founded on philosophical ideals. Living them takes understanding, not only of knowledge but also of ethics, principles, and virtues. Respect and tolerance of diverse solutions and propositions lead to greater understanding and respect—even if philosophical differences exist and remain.

WHAT CITIZENS MUST KNOW

- Civility does not restrain the expression of ideas: it simply has to do with the manner in which ideas are expressed.
- Instability and oppressing others in a despotic manner, even in defending virtuous principles, raises questions of character and ethics.
- Schools should address civility in words and actions and be primary models to students of civility.
- In actuality, intangibles—principles, values, and ethics—are the foundation for integrity, credibility, and civility.
- Students need to learn the importance of self-discipline, compassion, responsibility, friendship, hard work, courage, perseverance, honesty, and loyalty.

- Acting with integrity is not without conflict or criticism: it requires courage and fortitude to do what is ethical and moral.
- In short, wisdom is having a depth and breadth of knowledge and using it for the "greater good" of self and others.
- Citizens must be aware of and understand the three ethical perspectives: the "utilitarian" approach, the "rights" approach, and the "virtue" approach.

NOTES

1. Linda Fisher Thornton, "Civility Is an Ethical Issue," http://leadingin context.com/2012/08/08/civility-is-an-ethical-issue.

2. George A. Goens, *The Fog of Reform* (Lanham, MD: Rowman & Littlefield, 2016), 11.

3. William Bennett, *The Book of Virtues* (New York: Simon and Schuster, 2010).

4. Antonin Scalia, *Scalia Speaks: Reflections on Law, Phase, and Life Well Lived* (New York: Crown Publishing Group, 2017), 100.

5. George A. Goens, *It's Not My Fault: Victim Mentality and Becoming Response-able* (Lanham, MD: Rowman & Littlefield, 2017), 62.

6. George E. Vaillant, *Aging Well* (Boston: Little, Brown, 2003), 253.

7. Goens, *It's Not My Fault*, 57.

8. Scalia, *Scalia Speaks*, 25.

9. Manuel Valasquez, Claire Ander, Thomas Shanks, and Michael J. Meyer, "Thinking Ethically," Markula Center for Applied Ethics, Santa Clara University, http://www.scu.edu/ethics/ethics-resources/ethical-decision-making/thinking-ethically/.

12

EPILOGUE

The Foundation for a Civil Society

America is great because she is good. If America ceases to be good, America will cease to be great.

—Alexis de Tocqueville

Society can be brash as the coarseness increases and individuals respond in kind. Tolerating incivility as a given is not the solution because there is much at stake. Acceptance of destructive behavior is not an answer; neither is withdrawing into cocoons or silos. But what is the answer?

Sometimes adults can learn from children. Maybe adults should turn the tables and ask children how to treat and live with others. There might be a lesson there.

I asked Julia Goens, an eight-year-old third-grader, and Eddie, her seven-year-old brother, about how people should be treated. Eddie shouted, "Fair." Julia said, "Nicely! I don't want to be bullied or called names. I want people to be kind so no one's feelings get hurt." Clean and simple! No bullying. Kindness and being nice is what they want and what they give.

Going further, I asked the same question of Claire Bower, a high school senior. She responded, "I think the concept of listening to understand, rather than listening to respond, applies today. We need more understanding of each other, of peoples' histories, cultures, religions, traditions, and more in order to collaborate, compromise, and work together despite the differences that will always inevitably exist.

"I believe that our society has gotten too caught up in labels, and in our efforts to find united groups we feel we personally belong to, we have built walls within our society as we categorize ourselves into smaller populations that believe, think, and act differently. While it is important for us to all find a sense of self, belonging, and personal security, I think we all need to bear in mind that at the end of the day we are just people. Regardless of race, religion, sexuality, gender identity, etc. We are all just people. We are all trying to live the life we believe we need to live. I think it would all do us good to try to understand and respect others even if we don't personally agree with them."

In both cases, students, despite their age difference, highlight what is necessary for a more civil society, from simple kindness to a more mature understanding that listening and not labeling people and appreciating differences are basic essentials.

Labels really do not define people any more than our eye color does. People are more complex than that and don't always fit into a preconceived mold. The incessant categorization and lumping of people creates divisions and separation. Behind the external façade of personal appearance, people are simply human beings with the same needs.

People's personal stories, however, matter because they define them and their attitudes and perceptions. Even though stories differ, people can still be united around and respect the nation's core values. Different people coalesce around common values.

"We the people" is a descriptor that is based on the ideals of justice, liberty, equality, goodness, and freedom. Commitment to these ideals is more important than superficial demographic or political categories used to separate people, not bind them together.

Generational differences are interesting and expose different perspectives and possibly values. Older generations are experienced in facing and living life and everything it brings. The viewpoint of today's youth comes without the experience of confronting the vagaries of life. Complexities of life exist, and there are nuances to people's perspectives that move far beyond labels and slogans.

However, for all, the road of life is not straight. It is filled with curves, risky terrain, and some dead ends. Occasionally there are speed limits, stop signs, and an isolated flat tire or breakdown. Some are the result of choices, and others are the impact of fate.

Traversing the road takes toughness and resilience. Individuals, both young and old, cannot expect the course to be cleared for them. Failure is inevitable. Victories, large and small, arise. Sadness is unavoidable. Life involves unexpected circumstances and serendipity. The range of feelings is wide because people are human and emotion cannot, in reality, be suppressed.

Youth become able to vote at the age of eighteen. Think of that. One of the biggest responsibilities of adulthood and citizenship is actively and knowledgeably participating in government. While education prepares individuals for other facets of life, like employment and success, individuals at eighteen must jump into the full responsibilities of citizenship even though some have not yet graduated from high school. That is why educating to prepare for civic duties is important.

Values and principles are absolutely critical. They sculpt life and create a clear picture or image of what ought to be and what ought not to be. For all people, they provide the ballast in facing difficult and sometimes tragic times.

For the British during World War II's Dunkirk or for Americans at Pearl Harbor, commitment to protecting the nation's values and serving the common good of the country were tremendous uniting forces. In more contemporary times, September 11 highlighted the need to stand together on principle and work to overcome a great tragedy and an uncertain future.

Education must emphasize values and principles so that citizens comprehend and understand them, to ensure they are met with integrity and wisdom. In a metaphorical sense, values and principles are the engine that drives citizens down the road of history on a moral and ethical course. They provide the map and motivation leading to a "good" life and future with honesty and integrity as citizens pursue freedom and equality.

In a similar vein, individuals want to be "good" citizens, parents, and models. "Goodness" is an ideal—a virtue—that is a general marker for character. Living ethically and morally with values and principles is what "good" citizens do to maintain a "good" country. Justice, equality, and truth are principles and indicators of a "good" society that values life and liberty.

THINKING—AGAIN

Philosophy and ideas are at the core of both private and public life. The ability to sort fact from fiction, truth from distortion, and reason from ignorance are imperative for all citizens. It's also a big task for individuals with limited schooling or for youth who lack experience and extensive education.

Falsehoods exist on all sides of the political and social spectrum. Distortions of individuals and groups exist, and being able to see through them takes thought and research. Image making in the media surrounds everyone every day with politics, programs, and celebrity. Finding the path through the weeds of Madison Avenue imaging, misrepresentation, and propaganda requires strong thinking skills and astuteness. Skeptical and critical thinking are primary attributes of an intelligent citizenry.

Candor is refreshing, even though, at times, it can be difficult and straightforward with little regard for tone and sentiments. Truth can be direct and strident and rub beliefs, opinions, and feelings the wrong way. Citizens in a democracy do not need "safe spaces" away from disagreement and contemplation. Positions, even those that are bigoted or boorish, should raise counter-positions and ideas. Safety rests in reasoned responses, not in the restriction of free speech.

Raising the philosophical dissonance of those positions with American principles and ideals are part of a citizen's duty. Falling into a protective and passive safety shell is not a solution when silence can be interpreted as an affirmation of those positions.

Thinking involves principles and standing up for oneself while speaking up to ensure the veracity of principles and values. The fruit of a well-educated citizenry is seen in their character and contributions—including their social and political behavior.

Groups or organizations influence individuals. The United States affirms the importance of individuality and the contributions it makes to society. Americans have the freedom to be themselves, away from doctrinaire requirements or strict adherence to the philosophies of government officials. They just have to follow the rule of law.

Compliant thinking and pressure to conform are not in accordance with the country's foundation. Eleanor Roosevelt commented, "We are facing a great danger today—the loss of our individuality. It is besieged on all sides by pressures to conform: to a standardized way of living, to recognized—or required—codes of behavior, to rubber-stamp thinking. But the worst threat comes from within, from a man's or woman's apathy, his willingness to surrender to pressure, to 'do it the easy way,' to give up the one thing that is himself, his value and his meaning as a person—his individuality."[1]

Conforming to others' wishes and expectations, in a sense, diminishes a person's standing. Individuals must define and understand their own values and standards and convictions. They should not be imposed by others and govern their choices of what is expected or what is trivial. Succumbing to others' positions and standards compromises integrity.

Following rules of decorum are necessary to live together, but conforming to others' expectations is both dangerous and incompatible with a person's philosophy. Compromising one's integrity by selling out for acceptance or popularity destroys the honor and trustworthiness of the individual.

Citizens must stand up and live their convictions. The wisdom of the message, while not always popular, addresses a greater good, and can provide a positive example to others to stand up and be counted. Children must learn they have but one life to live, and they must live it with integrity and commitment to positive ideals and principles. Being true to oneself is possible only in a country that exists on the premise of life, liberty, and the pursuit of happiness.

In some cases, individuals avoid controversy for fear of criticism. Aristotle stated, "Criticism is something we can avoid easily by saying nothing, doing nothing, and being nothing."

CITIZENS AND CIVILITY

Citizenship is an extremely important role in creating a life of significance and living in a country and society that supports individuals in that pursuit. Civility to sustain national principles and to improve the future of the democracy is really up to an empowered people. There is no one else who is going to do it.

Coming together does not mean agreement. Reason and understanding guide the path to finding common ground and mutual respect. Debate ideas; don't castigate others for different opinions. Remember the First Amendment. Apply logic and critical and skeptical thinking to determine the core of issues, possible solutions, and, even, new perspectives that were not previously evident.

To do so, citizens need to be able to do several critical things, and schools must focus on them. Citizens must:

- Understand that in a democracy power rests with citizens and all must meet their civil responsibilities.
- Think in complex ways. Skeptical or critical thinking are essential to be able to analyze, synthesize, and evaluate ideas, principles, values, and ethical situations.
- Listen actively to comprehend the content and intent of messages but also to understand the reasons why people hold their convictions and ideas.
- Comprehend the difference between truth, opinion, and belief, understanding when a position is based on truth or is simply an opinion, belief, or ignorance.
- Engage in deliberation and dialogue to work with others civilly and find areas of common ground, creating deeper understanding of others' philosophies, background, and positions.
- Learn how to make the case for the position and be able to make the case for individuals with opposing positions, developing respect for opponents, as well as a deeper understanding of the issues.
- Understand constitutional rights, major American documents, and the role and operation of the government.
- Become informed by reading and examining reports and information from a variety of philosophical perspectives. Get outside the bubble. Read more than one newspaper—particularly newspapers with a different philosophical slant. Read a newspaper from another country to get another perspective.
- Exercise self-control. Remember that "enemyfying" is destructive, and acting in anger by intimidating, vilifying, or abusing others is destructive to all.
- Finally, think! Do not just go along. Howl in the wilderness to express truth, refusing to become just another sheep that goes along with the crowd. Engage!

President Dwight Eisenhower stated, "Politics ought to be the part-time profession of every citizen who would protect the rights and privileges of free people and who would preserve what is good and fruitful in our national heritage."

President Barack Obama stated, "Civility also requires relearning how to disagree without being disagreeable. Surely you can question my policies without questioning my faith or, for that matter, my citizenship."

NOTE

1. Eleanor Roosevelt, *You Learn By Living: Eleven Keys for a More Fulfilling Life* (New York: HarperCollins, 2011), 111.

BIBLIOGRAPHY

BOOKS

Adler, Mortimer J. *The Great Books of the Western World: A Lexicon of Western Thought; The Great Ideas.* New York: Macmillan, 1992.

———. *Paideia Problems and Possibilities.* New York: Macmillan, 1983.

———. *The Paideia Proposal: An Educational Manifesto.* New York: Macmillan, 1999.

———. *Ten Philosophical Mistakes.* New York: Macmillan, 1985.

Adler, Mortimer J., and Max Weismann. *How to Think about the Great Ideas: From the Great Books of Western Civilization.* Chicago: Open Court, 2001.

Badaracco, Joseph. *Leading Quietly: An Unorthodox Guide to Doing the Right Thing.* Boston, MA: Harvard Business School Press, 2002.

Bennett, William J. *Book of Virtues.* New York: Simon & Schuster Books, 1996.

Bishop, Bill, and Robert G. Cushing. *The Big Sort: Why the Clustering of Like-Minded America Is Tearing Us Apart.* Boston: Mariner Books, 2009.

Block, Peter. *Community: The Structure of Belonging.* S.l.: Berrett-Koehler, 2018.

Botstein, Leon. *Jefferson's Children: Education and the Promise of American Culture.* New York: Doubleday, 1997.

Bradley, Bill. *Time Present, Time Past: A Memoir.* New York: Alfred A. Knopf, 1996.

Burns, James MacGregor. *Leadership.* New York: Torchbooks, 1978.

———. *Transforming Leadership: The New Pursuit of Happiness.* New York: Atlantic Monthly Press, 2003.

Covey, Stephen R. *The 7 Habits of Highly Effective People: Restoring the Character Ethic.* New York: Rosetta Books, 2012.

Crosby, Barbara C., and John M. Bryson. *Leadership for the Common Good: Tackling Public Problems in a Shared-Power World.* San Francisco: Jossey-Bass, 2005.

Csikszentmihalyi, Mihaly. *Flow: The Psychology of Optimal Experience.* New York: Harper-Collins, 2008.

Etzioni, Amitai. *The Common Good.* Hoboken, NJ: Wiley, 2014.

———. *The New Golden Rule: Community and Morality in a Democratic Society.* New York: Basic Books, 1996.

———. *The Spirit of Community.* New York: Crown, 1993.

Fenton, Tom. *Bad News: The Decline of Reporting, the Business of News, and the Danger to Us All.* New York: Regan Books, 2005.

Fisher, Roger, and Roger Brown. *Getting Together: Building Relationships as We Negotiate.* Benjamin Publishing Group, 1989.

Foer, Franklin. *World without Mind: The Existential Threat of Big Tech*. New York: Penguin Publishing Group, 2017.

Galbraith, John Kenneth. *Affluent Society*. Boston: Houghton Mifflin, 1998.

———. *The Affluent Society and Other Writings, 1952–1967*. New York: Literary Classics of the United States, 2010.

Gardner, Howard. *Truth, Beauty, and Goodness Reframed: Educating for the Virtues in the Twenty-First Century*. New York: Basic Books, 2011.

Gardner, John W. *Excellence*. New York: W. W. Norton, 1984.

———. *Living, Leading, and the American Dream*. San Francisco: Jossey-Bass, 2003.

———. *The Recovery of Confidence*. New York: Norton, 1970.

Goens, George A. *The Fog of Reform*. Lanham, MD: Rowman & Littlefield, 2016.

———. *It's Not My Fault: Victim Mentality and Becoming Response-able*. Lanham: MD: Rowman & Littlefield, 2017.

———. *The Promise of Living*. San Francisco: Turning Stone Press, 2013.

———. *Soft Leadership for Hard Times*. Lanham, MD: Rowman & Littlefield, 2005.

Goens, George A., and Phil Streifer. *Straitjacket*. Lanham, MD: Rowman & Littlefield, 2013.

Goleman, Daniel. *Emotional Intelligence*. New York: Random House, 2012.

Hart, Gary. *The Good Fight*. New York: Random House, 1993.

———. *The Republic of Conscience*. New York: Blue Rider Press, an Imprint of Penguin Random House, 2015.

Havel, Vaclav. *The Art of the Impossible*. New York: Knopf, 1997.

Hirsch, E. D. *The Schools We Need and Why We Don't Have Them*. New York: Doubleday, 1996.

Isaacs, William, and Peter M. Senge. *Dialogue and the Art of Thinking Together: A Pioneering Approach to Communicating in Business and in Life*. New York: Currency Publishers, 1999.

Jacoby, Susan. *The Age of American Unreason in a Culture of Lies*. New York: Vintage Books, 2009.

Kahane, Adam, and Jeff Barnum. *Collaborating with the Enemy: How to Work with People You Don't Agree with or Like or Trust*. Oakland, CA: Berrett-Koehler, 2017.

Kellerman, Barbara. *Bad Leadership: What It Is, How It Happens, Why It Matters*. Boston: Harvard Business Review Press, 2014.

Kofman, Fred. *Authentic Communication: Transforming Conversation in the Workplace*. Boulder, CO: Sounds True, 2014.

———. *Conscious Business: How to Build Value through Values*. Boulder, CO: Sounds True, 2014.

Levin, Yuval. *The Fractured Republic: Renewing America's Social Contract in the Age of Individualism*. Updated with a new epilogue. New York: Basic Books, 2017.

Lynch, Michael Patrick. *True to Life: Why Truth Matters*. Cambridge, MA: MIT Press, 2005.

Mondale, Sarah, and Sarah B. Patton. *School, the Story of American Public Education*. Boston: Beacon Press, 2001.

Nathanson, Stephen. *Patriotism, Morality, and Peace*. Lanham, MD: Rowman & Littlefield, 1993.

Nichols, Tom. *The Death of Expertise: The Campaign against Established Knowledge and Why It Matters*. New York: Oxford University Press, 2017.

Palmer, Parker J. *Healing the Heart of Democracy: The Courage to Create a Politics Worthy of the Human Spirit*. San Francisco, CA: Jossey Bass, 2014.

Peterson, Christopher, and Martin E. P. Seligman. *Character Strengths and Virtues*. New York: Oxford University Press, 2004.

Postman, Neil. *Amusing Ourselves to Death: Public Discourse in the Age of Show Business*. New York: Penguin, 2005.

Ravitch, Diane. *Reign of Error: The Hoax of the Privatization Movement and the Danger to America's Public Schools*. New York: Knopf Doubleday, 2013.

Roosevelt, Eleanor. *You Learn By Living: Eleven Keys for a More Fulfilling Life*. New York: HarperCollins, 2011.

Scalia, Antonin, and Bryan A. Garner. *Making Your Case: The Art of Persuading Judges*. St. Paul, MN: Thomson/West, 2008.

Scalia, Antonin, Christopher J. Scalia, and Edward Whelan. *Scalia Speaks: Reflections on Law, Faith, and Life Well Lived.* New York: Crown Forum, 2017.

Schlesinger, Arthur M. *Disuniting of America: Reflections on a Multicultural Society.* New York: W. W. Norton, 2007.

Sergiovanni, Thomas J. *Moral Leadership: Getting to the Heart of School Improvement.* San Francisco, CA: Jossey-Bass, 1992.

Vaillant, George. *Aging Well.* Boston: Little, Brown, 2002.

———. *The Wisdom of the Ego.* Cambridge, MA: Harvard University Press, 1993.

Wolfe, Alan. *Return to Greatness: How America Lost Its Sense of Purpose and What It Needs to Do to Recover It.* Princeton, NJ: Princeton University Press, 2005.

PERIODICALS, BLOGS, AND REPORTS

Annenberg Public Policy Center. "Americans Are Poorly Informed about Basic Constitutional Provisions." September 12, 2017. https://www.annenbergpublicpolicycenter.org/americans-are-poorly-informed-about-basic-constitutional-provisions/.

Carnegie Corporation of New York and CIRCLE. "The Civic Mission of Schools." Carnegie Corporation and Center for Information and Research on Civic Learning and Engagement.

Carr, Nicholas. "How Smartphones Hijack Our Minds." *Wall Street Journal*, October 6, 2017.

Carter, Jimmy. "The Public Papers of the Presidents, 1977." Washington, DC: Government Publishing Office, 1978, 1980.

"Civil Liberties and Civil Rights." American Government online. http://www.ushistory.org/gov/1-.asp.

cmrubinworld.com. "Global Search for Education: Reimagining Learning on July 4 with Dr. Howard Gardner." 2017.

Douglass, Frederick. "Speech: National Convention of Colored Men, Louisville, Kentucky, September 24, 1883." http://coloredconvention.org/items/show/554.

Epstein, Mark. "The Google-Facebook Duopoly Threatens Diversity of Thought." *Wall Street Journal*, December 18, 2017. https://www.wsj.com/articles/the-google-facebook-duopoly-threatens-diversity-of-thought-1513642519.

Facione, Peter A. "Critical Thinking: What It Is and Why It Counts." 2013. https://www.nyack.edu/files/CT_What_Why_2013.pdf.

Ferguson, Niall. "In Praise of Hierarchy." *Wall Street Journal*, January 6, 2018.

Flowers, Betty Sue. "American Dream and the Economic Myth." *Huffington Post Blog*, Spring 2007.

Haidt, John. "The Age of Outrage." *Manhattan Institute*, November 15, 2017. https://www.manhattan-institute.org/html/2017-wriston-lecture-age-outrage-10779.html.

Hytten, Kathy. "Democracy and Education in the United States." *Oxford Research Encyclopedia of Education*, March 2017.

Katsanos, Tina, Vaughn Schmutz, Kendra Jason, Michelle Pass, and Honore Missihoun. "Promoting Professionalism in the Classroom." http://journal.uncc.edu/facultyguide/article/view/381/375/page2.

Kohn, Alfie. "Progressive Education: Why It's Hard to Beat, but Also Hard to Find." https://www.alfiekohn.org/article/progressive-education/.

Koppel, Ted. *Commencement Address*, May 1987. Duke University, Durham, NC. https://duke.edu/ark:/87924/r4d21rz7w.

Levine, Peter, and Kei Kawashima-Ginsberg. "The Republic Is (Still) at Risk and Civics Is Part of the Solution." Jonathan M. Tisch College of Civic Life, Tufts University, 2017. http://www.civxsummit.org/documents/v1/SummitWhitePaper.pdf.

Levinson, Meira. "Prepare Students to Be Citizens." *Phi Delta Kappan.* http://www.kappanonline.org/rd-prepare-students-citizens/.

McLean, Sam. "Politics of the Comment Good (blog)." October 2009. http://www.thersa.org/discover/publications-and-articles/rsa-blogs/2009/10/politics-of-the-common-good.

Minessence Group. "Once the Difference between Values, Ethics, in Principles?" https://values-knowledge-base.blogspot.com/2011/12/whats-difference-between-values-ethics.html.

Mitchell, Christopher R. "Conflict, Social Change and Conflict Resolution. An Enquiry." Berghof Research Center for Constructive Conflict Management. https://www.berghof-foundation.org/fileadmin/redaktion/Publications/Handbook/Dialogue_Chapters/dialogue5_mitchell_lead-1.pdf.

National Council for the Social Studies, 2013. http://www.socialstudies.org/sites/default/files/publications/se/6505/650511.html.

Patterson, Thomas E. "News Coverage of the 2016 General Election: How the Press Failed the Voters." Shorentstein Center on Media, Politics and Public Policy, December 7, 2016. https://shorensteincenter.org/news-coverage-2016-general-election/.

Pew Research Center. "Partisanship and Political Animosity in 2016." http://www.people-press.org/2016/06/22/partisanship-and-political-animosity-in-2016/.

———. "Patriotic, Honest, and Selfish: How Americans Describe . . . Americans." November, 2015. http://www.pewrescarch.org/fact-tank/2015/12/11/patriotic-honest-and-selfish-how-americans-describe-americans/.

———. "Sharp Partisan Divisions in Views of National Institutions." October 7, 2017. http://www.people-press.org/2017/07/10/sharp-partisan-divisions-in-views-of-national-institutions/.

Porath, Christine, and Christine Pearson. "The Price of Incivility." *Harvard Business Review* (January–February 2013), R13013.

Roosevelt, Eleanor. "Good Citizenship: The Purpose of Education." *Eleanor Roosevelt Papers Project*, George Washington University. https://www2.gwu.edu/~erpapers/documents/articles/goodcitizenship.cfm.

Roosevelt, Theodore. "The Duties of American Citizenship." New York: Buffalo, January 26, 1883. http://gle.yale.edu/dutis-American-citizenship.

Schnur, Jon. "Can We Teach Kids to Be Good Citizens?" *Time*, December 6, 2011. http://Time.com/2011/12/06/can-we-teach-kids-to-be-good-citizens.

Shandwick, Weber, and Powell Tate. KRC Research. "Civility in America VII: The State of Civility." http://www.webershandwick.comuploads/news/files/civility_in_america_the_state_of_civility.pdf.

"SPJ Code of Ethics." *Society of Professional Journalists*. https://www.spj.org/ethicscode.asp.

Velasquez, Manuel, Claire Andre, Thomas Shanks, and Michael J. Meyer. "The Common Good." *Issues in Ethics*, Spring 1992. http://scu.edu/ethics.resources/ethical-decision-making/the-common-good/.

———. "Thinking Ethically." Markula Center for Applied Ethics, Santa Clara University. http://www.scu.edu/ethics/ethics-resources/ethical-decision-making/thinking-ethically/.

Watts, Duncan J., and David M. Rothschild. "Don't Blame the Election on Fake News. Blame It on the Media." *Columbia Journalism Review*, December 5, 2017. https://www.cjr.org/analysis/fake-news-media-election-trump.php.

Wegner, Daniel M., and Adrian F. Ward. "The Internet Has Become the External Hard Drive for Our Memories." *Scientific American*, December 1, 2013.

"Why We Still Need Public Schools: Public Education for the Common Good." Center on Education Policy. http://cep-dc.org.

INDEX

ABOUT THE AUTHOR

George A. Goens, PhD, has written six books and coauthored four on leadership, school reform, education, and social issues. He served in teaching positions and as an executive as well as a leadership consultant to public boards and individuals.

CPSIA information can be obtained
at www.ICGtesting.com
Printed in the USA
LVHW091533280619
622665LV00008B/72/P